Eat, Drink & Be Merry

A Christmas Miscellany

❄

Eat, Drink & Be Merry

A *Christmas* Miscellany

SUSAN KELLEHER & RENÉ RODGERS

ENGLISH HERITAGE

Published by English Heritage, Isambard House, Kemble Drive, Swindon SN2 2GZ
www.english-heritage.org.uk

English Heritage is the Government's statutory advisor on all aspects of the historic environment.

Copyright © English Heritage
Text © Susan Kelleher and René Rodgers

Every effort has been made to trace copyright holders and we apologise in advance for any unintentional omissions, which we would be pleased to correct in any subsequent edition of this book.

The chapter opener images are as follows: choristers at Winchester Cathedral in the late 1970s (p 6); a Christmas display made entirely of lard and various meats at Smithfield Market in 1928 (p 26); avoiding a hangover at a Christmas party in 1955 (p 64); and the keepers and animals at Regent's Park Zoo celebrate Christmas in 1952 (p 86).

First published 2007

10 9 8 7 6 5 4 3 2 1

ISBN 978 185074 961 5
Product code 51180

British Library Cataloguing in Publication data
A CIP catalogue for this book is available from the British Library.

Edited by Adèle Campbell, English Heritage Publishing
Brought to press by Susan Kelleher and René Rodgers, English Heritage Publishing
Designed by Andrew Barron, Thextension
Printed in Belgium by Deckers-Snoeck

Contents

Introduction

The 12 days of Christmas represent many things. For some they are first and foremost a religious festival, for others a chance to get that new red bike, for many an excuse to over-indulge, and for most a much-deserved few days off work. For some the whole experience is painful and best avoided. But whatever its significance, few of us give much thought to the history of Christmas, to the origins and development of its many traditions.

Most of the elements of today's Christmas festivities are Victorian inventions or revivals, though many have their origins in the pagan past and some have evolved with distinct regional or national variations. Detailed studies of the subject have filled larger books than this – you'll find some such volumes listed in our Further Reading – and much of the information available on the subject is contradictory and inconclusive. *Eat, Drink and Be Merry* doesn't claim to be the authority on the subject but instead offers a celebratory selection – as subjective and gratuitous as Christmas itself. It's something to dip into when that last turkey sandwich has rendered Twister impossible; light enough to nibble at when you thought you couldn't possibly manage another thing. It's filled with historical highlights, facts, legends, recipes and anecdotes – new interpretations of familiar

CHARLES DICKENS' *A Christmas Carol*, published in 1843, emphasised the charitable side of Christmas. That year over 15,000 copies of his story were sold and it appeared as a play in nine London theatres in 1844.

things and much more that will surprise you and make you smile. As the title suggests the miscellany covers everything from goose to punch to panto (a fairly typical sequence of events in many festive homes); but, of course, there is more to Christmas than its outer trimmings.

As the season becomes increasingly commercial, with shops putting up their displays and decorations as early as September, Christmas can feel like a very secular affair and the season's religious origins and traditional sentiments of peace and goodwill are easily forgotten. While Christmas has its pagan precursors – winter festivals that had been celebrated since prehistoric times – its origins as a Christian festival lie in the story of the nativity, and the development of the Christmas tradition grew out of a desire to mark the birth of Jesus Christ in the Christian calendar. So the best introduction to Christmas is to retell the most famous story of them all, and that is where this miscellany begins. ❉

9

TWO BOOKS OF THE NEW TESTAMENT – the gospels of St Matthew and St Luke – provide the familiar elements of the birth of Christ although they focus on different aspects of the tale. Luke records the angel Gabriel's visit to Mary, the Holy Family going to Bethlehem and the shepherds coming to see the Christ child, while Matthew tells us about the angels' revelations to Joseph and the story of the wise men and King Herod. Interestingly, neither of the other gospels record Jesus's birth or childhood at all and some of the accepted details of the story aren't actually recorded by Matthew or Luke. While the Bible provides us with the bare bones of Christ's birth, the story has been embroidered by later writers and scholars who have attempted to fill in some of the blanks by relating the events to what we know about the history of the period. This combination of religious faith, historical facts and interpretation thus came together to form the familiar story of the nativity.

10

A young girl called Mary who lived in Nazareth was betrothed to Joseph. Before they were married, God's messenger appeared to her in the form of the archangel Gabriel and revealed that she would bear the Son of God. Mary was naturally amazed at this news as she was still a virgin, but Gabriel assured her that she was highly favoured by God and that the intervention of the Holy Ghost would make this possible. In Christianity, this revelatory moment is known as the Annunciation.

Joseph was shocked when he learnt of Mary's pregnancy and felt unable to marry her – although he decided to end their relationship privately rather than make a public example of her. But he changed his mind after having a dream in which an angel told him that Mary's child had been conceived by the Holy Ghost. The angel announced to Joseph that 'she shall bring forth a son, and thou shalt call his name Jesus: for he shall save his people from their sins' (Matthew 1:21).

When Mary was heavily pregnant Augustus, who was Roman emperor from 27 BC until AD 14, ordered a census for the purposes of taxation; in Judea this meant that everyone had to travel to the cities and towns of their ancestral tribes to register for this taxation. So Joseph and Mary left Nazareth and went to enrol in Bethlehem – the city of David – as Joseph was from the 'house and lineage of David'. When they arrived, Bethlehem was so overcrowded that they couldn't find anywhere to stay. The tradition is that they eventually found space in a stable and it was there, in the company of animals, that Mary gave birth to her son. (However, the Apocryphal Gospels record that Jesus was born in a cave and the Bethlehem Tourist Board seems to agree!)

Around this time a group of shepherds, who were watching over their flocks nearby, were startled by the appearance of an angel who said, 'Fear not: for, behold, I bring you good tidings of great joy, which shall be to all people. For unto you is born this day in the city of David a Saviour, which is Christ the Lord. And this shall be a sign unto you; Ye shall find the babe wrapped in swaddling clothes, lying in a manger' (Luke 2:10–12). The sky was then filled with angels proclaiming, 'Glory to God in the highest, and on earth peace, goodwill toward men' (Luke 2:13–14). With this sign from God, the shepherds went to Bethlehem and found Mary, Joseph and the baby just as the

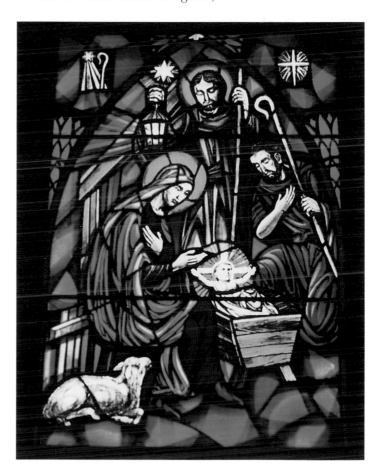

angel had described and then spread the good news of the Saviour's birth to everyone they met.

After Jesus was born 'wise men from the east' came to Judea searching for the King of the Jews, navigating their journey by following a star, which later writers called the Star of Bethlehem. When Herod, who had been made king of Judea by the Roman Senate in 40 BC, heard about their search he asked his advisors where this new 'king' would be born and they recounted the prophecy about the birth of Christ: 'And thou Bethlehem, in the land of Juda, art not the least among the princes of Juda: for out of thee shall come a Governor, that shall rule my people Israel' (Matthew 2:6). Herod, threatened by the idea of a King of the Jews who might challenge his authority, conspired to find out exactly where the baby could be found by asking the wise men to go to Bethlehem and then bring word to him so that he too could worship the child. The star duly led them to Bethlehem and here they found the house where the family was now living and, as Matthew says, they 'fell down, and worshipped him: and when they had opened their treasures, they presented unto him gifts; gold, and frankincense and myrrh' (Matthew 2:11). Because the wise men had each been warned in a dream that they should not reveal the baby's whereabouts to Herod, they went home by another route. At the same time an angel told Joseph to flee into Egypt with Mary and Jesus, and to remain there until he heard that it was safe to return. They escaped just in time as Herod, determined to prevent the rise of a new king, ordered the murder of all male children in Bethlehem who were two years old and under, an event that is known as the Massacre of the Innocents.

This is the basic story of the birth of Jesus, but how did the actual festival of Christmas come about?

———————

OPPOSITE
Detail of the painted ceiling by Antonio Belluci, 1720, in the Church of St Michael, Witley, Worcestershire.

We three kings...

Matthew does not give us much information about the wise men and, indeed, he does not even record that there were three of them though this has become the traditional image in depictions of the nativity, perhaps based on the number of gifts that were given to Jesus. They are simply called wise men in the gospel of Matthew, but they have also been called Magi or the Three Kings by later writers. According to the Greek historian Herodotus the Magi were a priestly caste from the Median Empire, while in the Christian tradition the Magi are sometimes viewed as Zoroastrian astrologers from ancient Persia (Zoroastrianism was a pre-Islamic monotheistic religion that originated in Persia). Their interest in astrology could explain why the wise men followed the so-called Star of Bethlehem in order to find Jesus. Indeed, it wasn't uncommon for stellar events to be linked to major figures or happenings at this time. Interestingly, many scholars have tried to pin down a specific astronomical event to explain the star, such as a nova, a planet or a comet, with many focusing on a conjunction of Jupiter and Saturn in 7 BC.

The assumption that the wise men were kings was perhaps an interpretation made by early Christians from several references in the Old Testament, especially a passage from the Book of Psalms: 'The kings of Tarshish and of the isles shall bring presents: the kings of Sheba and Seba shall offer gifts' (72:10). However, it is also possible that the association of the wise men with kings came about later in order to create a relationship between them and Christian monarchs. Certainly various English kings and queens made a point of offering gifts of gold, frankincense and myrrh in a royal chapel on 6 January – Epiphany in the Christian calendar. (Epiphany commemorates, amongst other things, the visit of the wise men to the Christ child when they gave their gifts to him, though no specific date for this event is actually given in the Bible.)

14

The Adoration of the Magi by Andrea Vaccaro (c 1598–1670).

Despite not being individually described in the Bible, the wise men have been given names and countries of origin in western Christian tradition: Caspar (from Tarsus), Balthasar (from Ethiopia) and Melchior (from Arabia). Their gifts have been interpreted on two levels: firstly, the gifts themselves were valuable commodities in the ancient world and thus seen as being fit for a king; they have also been viewed as symbolic or prophetic with gold representing kingship, frankincense representing priesthood or divine authority and myrrh representing death due to its use as an embalming oil. There has also been speculation about what happened to the three wise men after their encounter with Jesus, with some commentators claiming that they were baptised by St Thomas when he was on his way to India and possibly later martyred for their faith. Helena, the mother of Constantine the Great (c AD 272–337), supposedly found the bodies of the three wise men while on pilgrimage to the Holy Land and took them home to Constantinople as important religious relics to be displayed in the church of Hagia Sophia. Later their bodies were allegedly moved to Milan and from there they were sent to Cologne by the Holy Roman Emperor, Frederick I, in 1163 or 1164. Today the Shrine of the Three Kings in Cologne Cathedral is said to contain their bones. However, Marco Polo's writings contradict this account, recording that he actually saw their preserved bodies – 'with hair and beard remaining' – in Persia while on his travels in the 13th century.

There is one final twist to the tale: in 2004 the Church of England declared that the latest prayer book would use the term Magi rather than wise men. They based this revision on the idea that Magi was the term used for Persian court officials and that 'the visitors [to Jesus and his family] were not necessarily wise and not necessarily men'.

Many countries still commemorate the journey of the wise men. Here, Flemish wise men enjoy a cup of tea.

The sacred and the profane

THE GOSPELS OF SAINTS MATTHEW AND LUKE record stories about the nativity, but neither gives an actual date for Christ's birth, though one might speculate that Jesus was actually born in the spring since the shepherds in Luke's gospel were out in the fields with their flocks at the time. Consequently there is much debate about the date of the event.

In the early years of Christianity, the birth of Christ probably wasn't marked to any great extent. The early church opposed the observation of the birthdays of saints and martyrs – including Jesus – as death days were considered more significant since these marked their 'heavenly birthdays', the dates when saints and martyrs passed from this earthly life to eternal life or died for their faith. An early theologian even condemned the celebration of Christ's birth as sinful because it likened him to a 'king pharaoh', something perhaps too reminiscent of the veneration of the pagan deities and political leaders of the time. Therefore, early Christians focused more on the Feast of the Manifestation at Epiphany (6 January), when Christ was visited by the wise men, and the celebration of Christ's death and resurrection at Easter.

MANY PEOPLE DISAPPROVE of abbreviating Christmas to Xmas; however, the X is actually derived from the Greek for the first letter of Christ's name.

The first evidence of a firm date being attributed to Christmas comes from Clement of Alexandria who records *c* AD 200 that some Egyptian theologians had assigned the date of Christ's birth as 20 May. Other early church scholars postulated a variety of other dates. However, in AD 221 Sextus Julius Africanus identified 25 December as Christ's birth date in his reference book, *Chronographiai*. By the mid-4th century Pope Julius I (AD 337–52) had declared 25 December as the 'true date of the nativity' and the first real record of Christ's birth being marked on this date in Rome is found in the Philocalus Calendar of AD 354. The acceptance of this date soon spread to other parts of the Roman Empire – from the 4th century onwards this date was used in every western calendar and had been accepted in Constantinople by AD 379, followed by many other eastern churches. Christmas had become a civil holiday by AD 529 with the Second Council of Tours declaring the 12 days between Christmas Day and Epiphany a holy festival in AD 566 or 567.

There are various theories as to why the church settled on 25 December as the date for Christ's birth. Some of these are theological such as the concept that, like many of the Old Testament prophets, Jesus would have died at an 'integral age' – in other words he would have died on the anniversary of either his conception or his birth. The church believed that he was conceived and died on the same day, which was seen as 25 March, and his birth date could thus be set as 25 December, nine months after his conception. This correlation of dates was consistent with the idea that the actual number of years lived by many prophets was a 'perfect' whole number. However, the most common explanation for the choice of 25 December is related to the pagan festivals that fell around the same time, prompting the Church to set Christ's birth date as 25 December in order to counter these pagan celebrations.

'YULE' was the name of a Scandinavian midwinter festival; the term was later introduced to England as an alternative name for Christmas.

17

Most significantly, the Natalis Invicti – the birth of Sol Invictus or the Unconquered Sun – was celebrated on 25 December, giving it a strong connection with the establishment of this date for the birth of Jesus. The festival of the sun god was introduced by the Roman emperor Elagabalus (c AD 203–22), though he associated it with the native Syrian sun god El Gabal, and it was at its most popular during the reign of Aurelian (AD 214–75), who made the worship of Sol Invictus into an official cult that was observed throughout the Roman Empire. Later emperors also established connections with Sol Invictus, especially Constantine the Great (c AD 272–337). Many of his coins bear the words 'Soli Invicto Comiti' (The unconquered sun companion (of the Emperor)) and represent him with the sun god's radiate crown. Constantine's Edict of Milan (AD 313) proclaimed the toleration of Christianity throughout the Roman Empire and his own ideology shifted in favour of the church as his association with Christianity developed – for example the radiate crown was replaced by the Christian Chi-Rho symbol on his later coinage. Interestingly, solar symbolism associated with Sol was sometimes used in the Christian representations of Jesus – for instance, a 3rd-century AD mosaic decorating a mausoleum beneath St Peter's in Rome bears the image of Jesus in the guise of Apollo-Helios/Sol Invictus, with radiate crown and riding in the sun god's chariot. Some early Christian writers also associated Christ's birth with the rebirth of the sun. John Chrysostom (AD 349–407), Archbishop of Constantinople, emphasised the connection between the festival of Sol Invictus and Christ

18

This 3rd-century AD mosaic in Rome depicts Jesus as the sun god.

when he wrote: 'But Our Lord, too, is born in the month of December... the eight before the calends of January [25 December]... But they call it the "Birthday of the Unconquered". Who indeed is so unconquered as Our Lord...? Or, if they say that it is the birthday of the Sun, He is the Sun of Justice.' Other Church fathers, however, felt compelled to stress that Sol was not the Christian god and that any association between the two was heretical.

Another Roman festival that may have influenced the date of Christmas is the Saturnalia – certainly some of the elements of its celebration can be found in many of our Christmas traditions. Saturnalia was observed for seven days from 17 December and focused on

Saturn, the god of agriculture, and the return of the sun. This was a period of extreme merrymaking with feasting, visiting friends and exchanging gifts such as wax candles and small earthenware figurines called *sigillaria*, processions, bonfires, decorating with greenery and role reversal all being commonplace (and all being traditions that were later embraced in Christmas celebrations). It was a very popular holiday with the Roman people and there is even reference to it in Roman Britain where one of the Vindolanda writing tablets refers to payment for items for a Saturnalia celebration. Catullus, a poet in the 1st century BC, described it as 'the best of days' and the 1st-century AD poet Martial wrote several epigrams to accompany gifts given at Saturnalia. However, other Roman observers apparently deplored some of its excesses, with the Stoic writer Seneca the Younger noting that '...loose reins are given to public dissipation...'. Soon after the end of Saturnalia, Romans turned their attention to the festival of the Kalendae, sacred to Janus and observed 1–3 January. Again, this was a period of feasting and gift-giving in order to bring good luck for the new year.

A Victorian representation of the Roman Saturnalia.

Other pagan observances fell in December, especially around the winter solstice. This was a natural time to celebrate as it was seen as the point when the worst of the winter was over and the sun was beginning to return. In fact, it was a common belief that the celebrations that marked the winter solstice would encourage the gods to bring fertility and light back to the land. In Scandinavia this period was known as Yule – a time of feasting and drinking – and lasted from 21 December through to January. The Venerable Bede (673–735) wrote that the Anglo-Saxons began their year on 'the 8th of the Kalends of January' (25 December) and that the important festival of Modranicht or Mother Night was held the night before; however, he does not give any further information about what this festival was specifically related to or how it was celebrated, and indeed it is possible that it was related to the observance of the Christian nativity (the Anglo-Saxons simply called this 'midwinter' until 1038).

While we do not know for sure why 25 December was chosen as the date of Christ's birth, there is clearly quite a lot of evidence that December was a time of celebration in the pre-Christian era. Some scholars believe that the Christian date may have been set in December in order to replace the existing pagan festivals and observances held around that time. Indeed, by placing Christmas in December and absorbing some elements of the earlier festivals, the Church's motivation could have been to facilitate acceptance of the Christian date and consequently make it easier to convert others to Christianity (facilitated by Constantine's encouragement of Christianity). Whatever the reasons, Christmas is now one of the most recognised dates in the calendar, embraced by people in many parts of the world as both a religious and secular holiday.

CHRISTMAS IS CELEBRATED on 7 January in some Eastern Orthodox churches – this is because they still adhere to the Julian calendar, which was replaced by the Gregorian calendar in 1582.

20

Highlights from the history of Christmas

★ THE NAME 'CHRISTMAS' was not actually seen in the written record until 1038, when it appeared in a Saxon text as the Old English *Cristes Maesse*, or 'the mass of Christ' – the church service that marked Christ's nativity. This mass consisted of three main services – one source records a midnight mass, a mass at dawn and a mass during the day, each with different liturgical focuses (for instance the midnight mass has been related to the angels in the nativity story, the dawn service to the visit of the shepherds to the Christ child and the day service to the actual coming of Christ). The Use of Sarum, a book of Christian ceremonies compiled at Salisbury Cathedral, records three masses on Christmas day itself with the first occurring right before dawn.

———

★ THE PATH OF CHRISTMAS did not always run smoothly. During the period of the English Civil War and the establishment of the Commonwealth (1642–60), Christmas was under siege by the Puritans. They viewed Christmas as a decadent time when many vices – such as drinking, gambling and feasting – were embraced and accepted, and they also deplored the relationship between Christmas and earlier pagan holidays. On a theological level, they believed that there was no scriptural basis for celebrating Christmas or anything in the Bible that supported 25 December as the date of Christ's birth, and thought that the veneration of the Holy Family had come about through papist influence.

Christmas as a holiday, along with all the traditional festivities, was actually banned by Parliament on 19 December 1644; in that year Christmas fell on a date set by law as a solemn fast day and so the order came that the fast must be observed and thus Christmas could not be celebrated. In the following years Parliament issued further restrictions against Christmas (and also Easter and Whitsun)

THE PURITANS OUTLAWED Christmas in Boston, USA, from 1659 to 1681. You could be fined 5 shillings for simply showing 'Christmas spirit'! Christmas also fell into decline after the American Revolution because it was viewed as an English tradition and it didn't become an official holiday in America until 1870.

celebrations. These included the restriction of church services, decorating with greenery and cooking special 'Christmas' dishes. On Christmas Day the shops were supposed to stay open and Parliament would be in session – in other words, it was supposed to be business as usual with no special marking of the day. The ban resulted in protests in many parts of England, some of these degenerating into Royalist uprisings, and a petition was signed by over 10,000 people in Kent stating that 'if they could not have their Christmas Day, they would have their King back on the throne'. Some people ignored the ban by continuing to celebrate in traditional ways. The Parliamentarian authorities reacted particularly fiercely against public displays – for instance, when the church of St Margaret's, Westminster, was decorated with greenery for a service, the churchwardens and preacher were arrested. John Evelyn was also arrested and questioned – along with the rest of the church's congregation – for attending a Christmas Day service in London in 1657. The Royalists responded to the ban and the related propaganda by producing their own pamphlets defending Christmas and ridiculing the Puritans for their extreme reaction to the holiday. A pamphlet entitled 'The Vindication of Christmas' of 1653 bears an illustration showing a bearded and robed Christmas being greeted by one person while being rejected by another. Though many people still celebrated Christmas in the privacy of their homes during this period, it wasn't until the restoration of the monarchy in 1660 and the return of Charles II that Christmas was once again celebrated publicly and the Puritans' restrictive legislation was overturned. Despite the ending of the

A Royalist pamphlet defending Christmas during the Puritan ban.

22

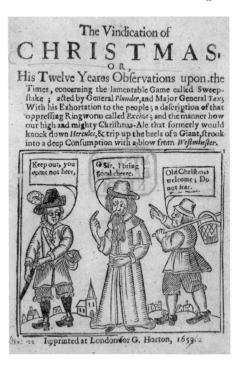

Christmas ban, however, it seems the level of celebration did not really return to the giddy heights of what it had previously been.

★ CHRISTMAS IN ENGLAND during the medieval and Tudor periods had stretched over quite a long period with the feasting and merrymaking often extending over the '12 days of Christmas'. And as noted, after the ban on Christmas had been lifted in 1660 the celebrations were more subdued. The celebration of the season changed further between 1790 and 1840 when employers (with the support of the government) began to cut into the traditional holidays of their workers in order to maximise production and profits. The Factory Act of 1833 stated that workers were only entitled to have Christmas Day and Good Friday off work (along with Sundays). And despite the Victorian love of Christmas, the Bank Holidays Act of 1871 only added one day – 26 December – as a formal Christmas bank holiday, meaning that there were now only two official days off over the Christmas period. Nevertheless, the Victorians did produce some more 'positive' social changes; for instance the Poor Law Board ordered that a special meal be provided in the workhouses on Christmas Day in 1847 and at a later date female paupers were given tea and sugar in order to make their day even more special! And despite the shortness of the official holiday, the Victorian period saw a real revival of Christmas as the Victorians looked nostalgically back at the way the holiday had been celebrated in the past and started to revive some old traditions and develop new ones. In fact, the Victorians are responsible for many of the elements of the Christmas festivities we know today.

Christmas charity in a Victorian workhouse.

23

A contemporary painting of the 1914 Christmas Day truce on the Western Front.

★ THE SPIRIT OF CHRISTMAS, peace and goodwill seems to have influenced First World War soldiers serving on the Western Front in France. In 1914 a spontaneous and unofficial truce was declared on Christmas Eve between some of the British and German soldiers. With the fighting temporarily stopped, both sides sang carols, exchanged Christmas greetings across the trenches and collected their recently fallen dead for burial, and there are even stories of gifts being swapped between the two sides and a football match being played between the opposing soldiers. Unfortunately spontaneous truces on this scale were actively prevented in the later years of the war by planned military actions on Christmas Eve.

Eat, Drink and Be Merry

★ THE SECOND WORLD WAR had a major impact on the actual celebration of Christmas. The Blitz and the enforced blackouts restricted the opportunities to travel to visit family and friends over the holiday, while rationing – which extended well into the 1950s – restricted the dishes that could be made as well as the presents that could be bought. Many people would carefully save their ration book coupons so they would be able to get the necessary ingredients to make at least some of the food that made Christmas so

special. At the same time, people were urged to spend their money on war bonds and National Savings Certificates in order to aid the war effort. And there was a common sentiment of celebrating Christmas as best you could so that – despite the hardship and the falling bombs – England could show her strength of character to the enemy. As a correspondent in a wartime *Picture Post* noted, 'And if we are merry at Christmas, we shall be showing the Nazis that we are winning the war of nerves, and maintaining the gallant spirit which has overcome the adversities which are no novelty to this windswept isle.'

HAPPY CHRISTMAS

Visé Paris 713

F. Mackin

'The same to you, and many of them!'

25

Eat

Sir Toby Belch:

…Does not our life consist of the
four elements?

Sir Andrew Aguecheek:

Faith, so they say; but I think it rather
consists of eating and drinking.

William Shakespeare, *Twelfth Night*, Act II, 1623

Many people would agree with Sir Andrew
and Christmas-time provides an excuse to
indulge even more. But eating is more than
just a pleasure – it has a symbolism that goes
back to our pagan origins.

As the Christian festival of Christmas developed it took on some of the popular pagan elements such as sacrificing an animal for the gods and enjoying a really good feast. These days we don't ceremoniously kill our turkey or goose, but there is still ritual involved in the way it is prepared and presented.

The enjoyment of food in connection with a sacred occasion is common throughout the world and in many different religions. For many people the eating and drinking associated with Christmas has become far more important than the religious observation of the festival.

Christmas food has long been rich and redolent with spices. It used to be a contrast to the food eaten at other times of the year and so the meal was eagerly anticipated and appreciated. It was, and still is, a more expensive meal that includes treats that cannot be afforded at other times of the year. Although the contents of the meal have varied over the centuries we still go to a lot of time, trouble and expense to ensure that it is special. We may not now have gilded peacocks and crowned swans for our Christmas dinner but our roast beef, ham or turkey is enjoyed just as much. ❄

The 14th Field Battery enjoying a Christmas party at Fort Brockhurst, Hampshire, in 1934.

THERE IS INVARIABLY ONE MAIN DISH THAT FORMS THE CENTREPIECE of the meal – in England that is now usually the turkey but other countries have different specialities. The turkey is, however, a relative newcomer to the festive board and other meat and poultry dishes were the 'dish of the day' in earlier times.

Boar's Head

BOAR ONCE ROAMED FERAL in Britain until they were hunted to extinction in the 13th century. There were various unsuccessful attempts in later centuries to reintroduce the species to Britain, but it is only recently that they are once again breeding in the wild as escapees from farms have established small herds.

Wild boar has long been a popular meat – in pagan times it was a sacred animal often used in ritual sacrifices and perhaps there is an element of these ancient rituals in the way the boar's head was later traditionally served at feasts to celebrate Christmas and other important occasions. With an apple or lemon wedged between its jaws and mounted on a silver platter, the head was paraded with great ceremony before the assembled company. As boar became increasingly difficult to obtain, its popularity as a Christmas centrepiece declined but it was still served in some households even in Victorian times.

———

IN NORSE MYTHOLOGY the god Freyr, who represented nature and fertility, owned an amazing gold boar named Gullinbursti (Golden Bristles), which shone so brightly it was able to turn night into day. At Yule, in deep midwinter, boar were sacrificed in Freyr's honour to ensure a plentiful harvest and the return of the sun. This legend may well be the reason why 17 December was known as Sow Day in the Northern Isles of Scotland. This was the day when every family that kept pigs would slaughter a sow.

———

31

SOME PLACES STILL SERVE THE BOAR'S HEAD at special dinners during December. The most famous is Queens' College, Cambridge, which holds an annual Boar's Head Gaudy a few days before Christmas. Attended by Old Members of the college, the boar's head is carried in to the hall, while a choir sings their version of the famous *Boar's Head Carol* which was published in 1521.

The boar's head in hand bear I,
Bedeck'd with bays and rosemary;
And I pray you, my masters, be merry,
Quot estis in convivio.
(So many as are at the feast.)

Caput apri defero
Reddens laudes Domino.
(The boar's head I bring
Giving praises to God.)

The boar's head, as I understand,
Is the rarest dish in all this land,
Which thus bedeck'd with a gay garland
Let us *servire cantico.*
(Serve with a song.)

Caput apri etc.

Our steward hath provided this
In honour of the King of bliss,
Which on this day to be served is
In *Reginensi Atrio.*
(In the Queen's Hall.)

Caput apri etc.

The story behind this custom is that a student of Queens' College was walking through woods one day absorbed in a book of Aristotle when an enormous boar charged him. With great presence of mind, the student waited until the boar was virtually upon him and then rammed the book deep into the animal's open jaws. The boar choked to death and the student hacked off its head – apparently keen not to lose his book. In triumph, he took the head back to the college where it was served up at the Christmas meal.

The Boar's Head procession at Queens' College, Cambridge.

———————

THE BOAR'S HEAD, IN ANCIENT TIMES, formed the most important dish on the table, and was invariably the first placed on the board upon Christmas day, being preceded by a body of servitors, a flourish of trumpets, and other marks of distinction and reverence, and carried into the hall by the individual of next rank to the lord of the feast.

Mrs Isabella Beeton, *Beeton's Book of Household Management*, 1861

———————

Swan and Peacock

THE MAGNIFICENT PLUMAGE of swans and peacocks was the main reason they were so often selected as the centrepiece at medieval banquets, particularly at Christmas. The meat in fact was pretty chewy, but the dish looked wonderful as both birds were cooked and served inside a cured skin, with the feathers from the head, body and tail kept for dressing.

Swans were the most expensive of the two, costing 3s 4d in 1380. They were the property of the Crown and any unauthorised person caught killing a swan was liable to severe punishment. The ownership of swans on the River Thames was extended to two livery companies in the 15th century – the Vintners and Dyers – but even as late as the 19th century anyone found guilty of taking a swan was likely to be sentenced to hard labour or transportation.

Swans were served on gold or silver platters and presented with their necks held upright and their wings swept back. They were decorated with a crown and garlands. Swans are still served occasionally today, for example the Vintners Company have a special swan dinner every November.

Peacocks were presented at table in a similar way with their head held up by a skewer, but their feathers were gilded. Peacocks were also served up in pies with the pastry shaped like the bird's body and the tail feathers added as decoration.

Swan Upping

During the ancient ceremony of Swan Upping, representatives of the Crown and the Vintners and the Dyers companies sailed along the River Thames to mark swans to signify ownership. The bills of the swans were nicked on one side to show they belonged to the Dyers, on both sides if they belonged to the Vintners and not at all if they belonged to the Crown. Cygnets were also taken to be fattened for the table.

Every July the pennant-festooned boats carrying uniformed officials of the Crown and the two livery companies still sail from Sunbury to Abingdon marking swans, but these days the swans and their cygnets are simply tagged round one of their legs.

The Queen still retains the right of ownership of all unmarked swans in open water, but in practice she only exercises this right on stretches of the River Thames and its tributaries.

34

Goose

GEESE HAVE BEEN PRIZED for thousands of years and were a popular meat in ancient Greece. They have long been bred all over the British Isles and fattened up for special occasions like Christmas. The high fat content, much of which leaches out during cooking, ensures a rich and succulent meat.

In the medieval period geese were one of the most popular Christmas dishes and goose remained a favourite until the late 19th century when it was usurped by the turkey. Nowadays goose is making a welcome comeback to the Christmas table.

———————

AS EVERYONE WANTED A GOOSE for Christmas but not everyone could afford one, special Goose Clubs developed in the 19th century so people could save up throughout the year. As these were often run from public houses, they were frowned upon by the Temperance Movement!

———————

AT CHRISTMAS THERE WOULD BE QUITE A QUEUE at the bakers – not for bread and cakes but for the use of the ovens to cook geese. Not everyone had ovens or if they did they were often not large enough to cook the Christmas goose.

THERE NEVER WAS SUCH A GOOSE. Bob said he didn't believe there was ever such a goose cooked. Its tenderness and flavour, size and cheapness, were the themes of universal admiration. Eked out by apple sauce and mashed potatoes, it was a sufficient dinner for the whole family; indeed, as Mrs Cratchit said with great delight (surveying one small atom of bone on the dish), they hadn't ate it all at last. Yet everyone had had enough, and the youngest Cratchits in particular were steeped in sage and onion to the eye-brows!

Charles Dickens, *A Christmas Carol*, 1843

GOOSE was also traditionally eaten at Michaelmas, the feast of St Michael and All Angels, celebrated on 29 September. Such was the demand for geese at this time that special Goose Fairs were held throughout the country. The famous Nottingham Goose Fair, which has been held since 1541, sold 20,000 geese from Lincolnshire and Norfolk. The fattened geese were herded all the way to Nottingham for the fair! Some Goose Fairs are still held – but you're more likely to enjoy a white-knuckle ride on a rollercoaster there than pick up your Christmas dinner.

GOOSE FAT is said to make the best ever roast potatoes to accompany your Christmas dinner.

DURING WARTIME RATIONING it was often difficult to obtain a goose for Christmas dinner so enterprising families made 'mock goose', a combination of lentils and vegetables, formed into the shape of a goose or cake (*see* opposite).

Turkey

THE TURKEY WAS UNKNOWN IN BRITAIN until the 16th century when William Strickland, who sailed with Sebastian Cabot on one of his voyages of discovery to North America, reputedly took a few back home with him. William Strickland bought estates at Boynton in Yorkshire and when he was rewarded with armorial bearings, he chose the turkey as part of his crest.

It was not until 1570 that there is a record of a turkey being eaten at a feast and turkeys remained expensive delicacies until the 17th century. Their popularity gradually increased but they did not become affordable until the 19th century. By the end of the 19th century the turkey was established as the firm favourite for Christmas dinner and by the late 20th century 89 per cent of people said that Christmas just wouldn't be Christmas without roast turkey.

TURKEYS WERE REARED AND FATTENED ON FARMS IN NORFOLK in the 18th century and sold at markets in London just before Christmas. The birds had to walk all the way to the capital to meet their fate and wore little leather bootees – or had their feet coated in tar – to protect their feet. After transport links improved in the 19th century, the turkeys were usually slaughtered on the farms and taken to London on coaches.

RIGHT
The turkey lectern at St Andrew's Church, Boynton, Yorkshire.

THE BACK OF THE LECTERN at St Andrew's Church in Boynton, Yorkshire, is carved in the shape of a turkey rather than the usual eagle. This was in memory of William Strickland who introduced turkeys to England in the early 16th century.

WHEN TURKEYS WERE INTRODUCED they were at first thought to be the same species as another edible bird recently brought in by merchants from the Near East. But when the two were seen to be different one had to be renamed. So the American bird remained turkie-fowl while the other was named after the place in West Africa where the traders had brought it from – guinea-fowl.

"MANY A TIME WE HAVE SEEN A NORFOLK COACH with its hampers piled on the roof and swung from beneath the body, and its birds depending, by every possible contrivance, from every part from which a bird could be made to hang. Nay, we believe it is not unusual with the proprietors, at this season, to refuse inside passengers of the human species in favour of these oriental gentry who 'pay better'."
William Hervey

CHRISTMAS CHEER

Christmas Greetings

Good husband and housewife, now chiefly be glad,
Things handsome to have, as they ought to be had.
They both do provide, against Christmas do come,
To welcome their neighbors, good cheer to have some.

Good bread and good drink, a good fire in the hall,
Brawn, pudding, and souse, and good mustard withal.
Beef, mutton, and pork, and good pies of the best,
Pig, veal, goose, and capon, and turkey well drest,
Cheese, apples and nuts, and good carols to hear,
As then in the country is counted good cheer.

What cost to good husband, is any of this?
Good household provision only it is:
Of other the like, I do leave out a many,
That costeth the husband never a penny.

Thomas Tusser (1524–80)

Vegetables and traditional accompaniments

EVERYONE HAS THEIR OWN FAMILY FAVOURITES but Christmas lunch or dinner is usually accompanied by one or all of the following:

STUFFING: Chestnut or sage and onion are traditional, but more exotic concoctions including fruit and other nuts are now becoming popular. The stuffing is placed in the neck end of the bird or cooked separately (often shaped into balls). It was known as forcemeat because it was forced into the bird.

SAUSAGES: Small sausages wrapped in strips of bacon are known as 'pigs in blankets'. When they are put round the roast turkey the dish is known as 'Alderman in Chains'.

VEGETABLES: Roast and mashed potatoes; roast parsnips; root vegetables such as carrots and swedes; green vegetables such as broccoli and, of course, the ubiquitous (and much maligned) Brussels sprouts.

CRANBERRY SAUCE/JELLY: Colonists arriving in North America in the early 17th century discovered wild cranberries as well as turkeys. They learnt how to cook both and found them a tasty combination. However, although the turkey soon became a popular Christmas meal, cranberry sauce took longer to be accepted and many people still prefer not to use it as they don't like the combination of sweet and savoury flavours.

BREAD SAUCE: Enjoyed for many centuries and reputedly part of medieval feasts, this thick sauce is a mixture of breadcrumbs, onion, bay leaf, cloves, mace, nutmeg, milk or cream and an optional dash of sherry.

The Brussels sprout

The Brussels sprout dates from the 13th century when it was grown not surprisingly in the region around Brussels in Belgium. It took several centuries before anyone was brave enough to eat it in England but, by the 18th century, it was a popular vegetable. If it is not boiled into a soggy, smelly mass, it is delicious – and has the added benefit of being full of vitamins, iron, potassium and fibre.

Puddings and Pies

FEW THINGS ARE RICHER THAN A TRADITIONAL CHRISTMAS PUDDING. The plum pudding is still the nation's favourite and it has a long history. Originally it wasn't a pudding at all but a sort of watery gruel made to various recipes with corn or oats, stock, fruit, sugar and spices (and sometimes eggs) that was traditionally eaten after the Advent fasting period. This dish was known as 'frumenty' or 'furmenty' after the Latin *frumentum* meaning corn and it is still enjoyed in some parts of the country.

By the 16th century this gruel was known as plum pottage and had become richer and thicker, and it developed into both a pudding and a cake (*see* p 59). The pudding ingredients were put into an animal intestine and boiled so it was rather like a sweet haggis, but this was a messy and labour-intensive process as intestines are awkward to clean properly. The introduction of the pudding cloth in the 17th century made life a lot easier as the ingredients could simply be wrapped up in the muslin. It also ensured that Christmas puddings were invariably round in shape.

Workmen in Oxford Street, London, warm up their Christmas pudding in an unconventional manner in December 1937.

Despite being banned by the Puritans, the Christmas pudding was too good to disappear from the Christmas table. By the early 18th century it was back and it has gradually become fruitier, and more alcoholic, over the years. The meat element declined and now only the suet remains.

———————

Wartime rationing meant that the luxury items needed to make Christmas pudding were unobtainable or at least very expensive. However the indomitable British housewife made do with what she could get hold of to ensure that the family still enjoyed a special treat.

War and Peace Christmas Pudding

8 oz (225 g) flour
8 oz (225 g) breadcrumbs
1 tsp bicarbonate of soda
1 tsp mixed spice
4 oz (100 g) suet
4 oz (100 g) dried fruit
8 oz (225 g) grated raw potato
8 oz (225 g) grated raw carrot

Mix all the ingredients together and put into a well-greased pudding bowl. The bowl should not be more than two-thirds full. Cover and boil or steam for 2 hours.

43

———————

How a Plum-Pudding was made in Paris

One of the French monarchs, wishing to show honour to the English ambassador on Christmas Day, gave orders that his cooks should make a plum-pudding for the foreign guest; and inasmuch as the cooks had no idea whatever of the way in which the eatable in question was to be fabricated, for they had never seen a plum-pudding before, perhaps scarcely ever heard of one, he sent to England for a recipe for the making of it.

The recipe came – so many raisins, so much suet, so much flour, etc. etc. Everything perfect. There could not possibly have been a better recipe given. This was handed over to the cooks, with strict injunctions not to deviate from it by one hair's breadth, to observe it with the most perfect accuracy. They did so – the weight of the ingredients,

their quality, the size of the copper in which it was to be boiled, the quantity of water, the duration of time – all was attended to. And the king spoke in dark, mysterious hints to the ambassador of some unknown gratification which was in store for him.

Well, at the appointed time in the dinner, up came the pudding. 'There,' said his majesty, 'mon ami. There! I have prepared a treat for you. There is your national dish, prepared in your national fashion. Eat and be merry.'

But the ambassador, instead of eating and being merry, only stared and rubbed his eyes. The plum-pudding was actually brought up in a tureen, and he was expected to eat it out of a soup-plate, like soup, with a spoon! The fact was, that though the king had had the best possible recipe sent him, and had had its injunctions most strictly attended to by his cooks, he had forgotten one little matter – he had omitted to tell them that it was to be boiled in a cloth.

The Leisure Hour, 30 December 1876

PUDDINGS AND PIES have always been associated with providing good fortune. The Christmas pudding often follows this tradition by including something silver in the mixture – a coin foretells wealth, a ring marriage and a thimble good luck to the person who finds them in their portion.

OH, A WONDERFUL PUDDING! Bob Cratchit said, and calmly too, that he regarded it as the greatest success achieved by Mrs Cratchit since their marriage.

Charles Dickens, *A Christmas Carol*, 1843

THE HACK OR HACKIN PUDDING is a speciality of Cumberland and the Lake District and it is traditionally eaten on Christmas morning. It is the earliest form of the Chrismas pudding, being an intestine stuffed with minced beef, dried fruit, sugar and oats.

45

AN ENGLISH GENTLEMAN at the opening of the great day – i.e., on Christmas Day in the morning – had all his tenants and neighbours enter his hall by daybreak. The strong beer was broached, and the blue-jacks went plentifully about, with toast, sugar, nutmeg, and good Cheshire cheese. The hackin (the great sausage) must be boiled by daybreak, or else two young men must take the maiden (i.e., the cook) by the arms, and run her round the market-place till she is ashamed of her laziness. In Christmas holidays the tables were all spread from the first to the last; the sirloins of beef, the minced pies, the plum porridge, the capons, turkeys, geese, and plum-puddings were all brought upon the board. Every one ate heartily, and was welcome, which gave rise to the proverb, 'Merry in the hall, when beards wag all.'

The Leisure Hour, 30 December 1876

———————

CHRISTMAS PUDDINGS, LIKE CHRISTMAS CAKES, should be made well in advance to allow the flavour to develop. The traditional day for making them is the Sunday before Advent, known as Stir-up Sunday from the Collect for that Sunday in the Church of England's *Book of Common Prayer*:

Stir up we beseech Thee, O Lord, the wills of Thy faithful people; that they, plenteously bringing forth the fruit of good works, may by Thee be plenteously rewarded, through Jesus Christ Our Lord. Amen.

———————

WHEN MAKING A CHRISTMAS PUDDING each member of the family is meant to give the pudding mixture a stir – and they should stir from east to west in honour of the wise men.

———————

46

The Reckoning

Now the festive season's ended
Comes the sequel parents dread;
Pale and visibly distended
Bilious Tommy lies in bed,
Face to face with retribution
And an outraged constitution.

What a change since, pink and perky,
Tommy swiftly put away
Three enormous goes of turkey
At the feast on Christmas Day,
Getting by judicious bluffing
Double quantities of stuffing.

As to pudding, who could reckon
Tommy's load in terms of size?
Who attempt to keep a check on
Tommy's numberless mince pies?
Hopeless task! His present pallor
Proves his prodigies of valour.

Then I found him, notwithstanding
Such colossal feats as these,
After dinner on the landing
Secretly devouring cheese,
Flanked by ginger-beer-and-coffee,
Sweetened with a slab of toffee.

I, his uncle, gave him warning,
Showed him the error of his ways,
Hinted at tomorrow morning,
Talked about my boyhood days;

All in vain I waved the bogey
He despised me as a fogey.

Well, perhaps the pains he suffers
May be gifts of fairy gold,
Since he now says, 'Only duffers
Eat as much as they can hold.'
Thus, through physic and privations,
Tommy learns his limitations.

Punch, 2 January 1907

Sonya Thomas, known as 'The Black Widow' on the competitive eating circuit, prepares for the Big Eat Mince Pie Eating Contest at Wookie Hole Show Caves, Somerset, in November 2006.

47

Eat, Drink and Be Merry

A CHEAP PLUMB PUDDING

Take 4 ounces of Flour, 4 ounces of Suet, 4 ounces of Raisins, a slice of brown bread, grate half a nutmeg, as much milk as will make it moist with 2 eggs – a spoonful of Brandy is an improvement & let it boil 5 Hours.

18th-century cookery book

———————

POURING WARMED BRANDY over the hot Christmas pudding and then setting it alight is a popular tradition. The pudding is enveloped in a blueish glow that signifies the all-encompassing love of Jesus.

———————

Mince Pies

PRESERVING MEAT WITH FRUIT AND ALCOHOL had been a common practice since medieval times and at Christmas this combination was used to fill pastry cases to make Christmas pies. These were usually rectangular as a reminder that Jesus was laid in a manger. They were made with minced meat which led to their name of minced or mince pies.

These too were banned by the Puritans in the 17th century as symbols of popery but they never lost their popularity. Gradually the meat element has declined and fruit and spices are now the main ingredients – though, as with the traditional Christmas pudding, suet is still used.

———————

YOU ARE SUPPOSED TO EAT a mince pie on each of the 12 days of Christmas to ensure 12 happy months the next year – although you'd probably suffer from indigestion for the first month!

———————

MINCE PIES WERE ALSO KNOWN AS SHRID PIES. The word is a derivation of 'shred' as the pies contained pieces of shredded meat.

———————

48

Jack Horner

Little Jack Horner
Sat in a corner
Eating a Christmas pie
He put in his thumb
And pulled out a plum
And said, 'What a good boy am I!'

This famous nursery rhyme is reputed to be a satire on the fortunes of Jack Horner who was the Steward of Richard Whiting, Abbot of Glastonbury, in the early 16th century. This was the period of the Dissolution of the Monasteries and the abbot was worried about the fate in store for Glastonbury, which was the richest abbey in the country and thus a prime target. He decided to send Henry VIII a 'sweetener' (literally!) in the form of a large Christmas pie (a mince pie) which he instructed Jack to take to the king. Partial as Henry VIII was to sweet things, the abbot knew that what would really put him in a good mood was the acquisition of property so he placed the title deeds of 12 manors inside the pie. But on the journey Jack 'put in his thumb' and pulled out one of the deeds for himself! Unfortunately 11 deeds were not a sufficient bribe and Richard Whiting was hanged, drawn and quartered on Glastonbury Tor and Glastonbury Abbey was destroyed. Meanwhile Jack Horner moved into the Manor of Mells where his family lived until the 20th century.

London's largest mince pie, donated to the children's ward of West London Hospital, Hammersmith, in December 1946.

49

Cheese

CHEESE HAS BEEN A STAPLE for thousands of years and though it is enjoyed as an everyday food it is also the perfect end to a delicious Christmas meal. The taste provides a foil for the rich flavours of traditional Christmas food as well as being an excellent accompaniment to port, brandy and other post-prandial tipples.

EVER SINCE THE ROYAL HOSPITAL, Chelsea, opened in 1692 the Ceremony of the Christmas Cheeses has been held on the first Wednesday in December. 'Cheese from Gloucestershire at 3d per lb' was the first Christmas cheese at Chelsea, but now a huge range is presented at the ceremony with cheeses being donated by makers from across the country. The event is held in the Great Hall where the cheeses are displayed with pride of place going to the huge Ceremonial Cheese – in recent years this has been a vast 54 lb Cheddar provided by the Montgomery family from Somerset. The cheeses are blessed by the chaplain and then one of the oldest Chelsea Pensioners cuts the Ceremonial Cheese with a sword.

Chelsea Pensioners at the Ceremony of the Christmas Cheeses, which is sponsored annually by the Dairy Council.

STILTON IS A POPULAR CHEESE that often graces the Christmas cheeseboard. The Stilton Cheesemakers' Association has created a range of healthy recipes that includes Stilton ice-cream!

IN PARTS OF SCOTLAND cheese was believed to have magical properties. *Caise Calluinn* (Christmas Cheese) was very special and one piece (the Laomacha) was left uneaten for good fortune. It was particularly prized if it had a hole in it because anyone lost on the hills only had to look through the hole to know exactly where they were – always assuming they had had the foresight to take the cheese with them!

———————

POETS HAVE BEEN MYSTERIOUSLY SILENT on the subject of cheese. Virgil, if I remember right, refers to it several times, but with too much Roman restraint. He does not let himself go on cheese. The only other poet that I can think of just now who seems to have had some sensibility on the point was the nameless author of the nursery rhyme which says: 'If all the trees were bread and cheese' – which is indeed a rich and gigantic vision of the higher gluttony. If all the trees were bread and cheese there would be considerable deforestation in any part of England where I was living. Wild and wide woodlands would reel and fade before me as rapidly as they ran after Orpheus. Except Virgil and this anonymous rhymer, I can recall no verse about cheese. Yet it has every quality which we require in an exalted poetry. It is a short, strong word; it rhymes to 'breeze' and 'seas' (an essential point); that it is emphatic in sound is admitted even by the civilization of the modern cities. For their citizens, with no apparent intention except emphasis, will often say 'Cheese it!' or even 'Quite the cheese.' The substance itself is imaginative. It is ancient – sometimes in the individual case, always in the type and custom. It is simple, being directly derived from milk, which is one of the ancestral drinks, not lightly to be corrupted with soda-water. You know, I hope (though I myself have only just thought of it), that the four rivers of Eden were milk, water, wine, and ale. Aerated waters only appeared after the Fall.'

G K Chesterton, from 'Cheese' in *Alarms and Discursions*, 1910

———————

Sweets and Treats

FOR EVERYONE WITH A SWEET TOOTH Christmas is a fantastic excuse to indulge it!

Soldiers fighting in the Crusades in the early 12th century tasted sugar for the first time and were immediately hooked. They brought back some of this unknown but very welcome addition to Britain's diet and demand grew so fast that trade in sugar quickly developed. Sugar was imported in the form of large cones which were known as 'loaves' and it was so expensive that it was kept under lock and key. Sugar was only used for very special occasions like Christmas and a wide range of 'sweet meats' were concocted to complement the savoury elements of the meal.

They were still served with the main feast but by the 17th century diners began to enjoy these sweet treats in a new way – the banqueting course. This banquet took place in another room and would consist of such sweet delights as marchpanes (marzipan moulded into intricate shapes and often painted and gilded); comfits (seeds coated with thick layers of sugar); cubes of sweet jelly (often coated in pure gold); and sugar plums (crystallised fruit). Gradually the appeal of going to a separate banqueting room declined but the popularity of the treats at the end of a meal remained. So the 'sweet' course developed and has remained the best part of a meal for many of us!

QUEEN ELIZABETH I enjoyed sugar so much that her teeth were black. This was a problem that affected much of the aristocracy who were the only people wealthy enough to afford sugar at this time.

SWEET CUBES OF JELLIED MILK were a Tudor delicacy which is rather like Turkish Delight.

A WHITE LEACH

Take a quart of newe milke, and three ounces weight of Isinglasse, half a pound of beaten suger, and stirre them togther, and let it boile half a quarter of an hower till it be thicke, stirring them al the while: then straine it with three sponfull of Rosewater, then out it into a platter and let it coole, and cut it in squares. Lay it faire in dishes, and lay golde upon it.

Thomas Dawson, *The good huswifes Jewell, part* 2, 1597

THE MODERN EQUIVALENT OF THIS RECIPE IS:

1 pint (575 ml) milk

5 tsps gelatine

4 oz (100 g) sugar

5 tsps rosewater

Put 4 tablespoons (60 ml) of the milk into a cup and then sprinkle the gelatine over it. Leave for 5 minutes before standing the cup in hot water and stirring the gelatine until it completely dissolves. Warm the remaining milk, stir in the gelatine and sugar and simmer, stirring continuously, for 5 minutes. Remove from the heat, stir in the rosewater and pour into a shallow baking dish about 6 in (15 cm) square which has been freshly rinsed in cold water. Allow to set firmly in a cool place before cutting into squares with a sharp knife.

––––––––––

ON CHRISTMAS EVE IN WALES a special toffee known as taffy is made to while away the hours before the service of Plygain (*see* p 148). Spoonfuls of the hot liquid toffee are put in saucers of cold water. The shapes formed by the setting toffee are meant to show the initials of the future spouses of unmarried members of the family.

––––––––––

54

ALMONDS HAVE BEEN AN IMPORTANT PART OF OUR DIET since medieval times. They are used in many different ways but one of the most popular at Christmas is as marzipan.

The city of Lübeck in Germany has long been famous for producing marzipan. It was an important trading centre in the Middle Ages when it was known as the Queen of the Hanseatic League because of its unique and vital position on the Baltic Sea. Merchants then brought marzipan to Britain where it was first sold in chemists as a remedy for impotence!

THE NIEDEREGGER FACTORY in Lübeck produces arguably the best marzipan in the world. At the factory life-size statues of the people who have played key roles in the company's history are displayed – all made out of marzipan!

CHOCOLATE IS SUCH A UNIVERSAL favourite and so versatile that it is invariably around in one form or another at Christmas celebrations. It is shaped into angels, fairies, snowmen etc and then wrapped in brightly coloured foil to form tree decorations; it is used to make chocolate log cakes; it can be served in a chocolate fountain etc. And boxes of chocolates and other sweets are always a popular Christmas present for young and old alike.

Twelfth Night Cake

EPIPHANY IS THE TWELFTH DAY OF CHRISTMAS and is celebrated on 6 January to mark the visit of the wise men to Jesus, as well as the end of Christmas. However, many people assert that Twelfth Night is actually 5 January as Christmas begins on sunset of 24 December.

Twelfth Night was party night. Ever since medieval times it was marked by a great feast and revels incorporating disguises and role reversals. A most important part of the festivities was a great cake which contained a dried bean – everyone took a slice and whoever got the bean was pronounced King of the Bean and they could order whatever they wanted! So servant could control master in a topsy-turvy world! At grand parties the cake was baked with a pea in one side and a bean in the other. Guests were given an appropriate slice from the cake and whoever had the bean was the King and whoever got the pea was his Queen. This drawing for a King and Queen is said to date back to the Roman Saturnalia. Cakes had other things baked into them which were meant to be reflections on the character of whoever drew them. On 6 January 1666 Samuel Pepys wrote in his diary: 'My wife to fetch away my things from Woolwich, and I back to cards and after cards to choose King and Queene, and a good cake there was, but no marks found; but I privately found the clove, the mark of the knave, and privately put it into Captain Cocke's piece, which made some mirthe, because of his lately being knowne by his buying of clove and mace of the East India prizes.'

The impressive Twelfth Night cakes had developed from the simple fruit and

A 1931 magazine cover showing *La Fête du Roi*, the French equivalent of the Twelfth Night celebrations.

57

oatmeal porridge that had been eaten in earlier periods (*see* p 42). The addition of flour, eggs and butter transformed the porridge into a cake that was usually cooked by boiling as only rich households had a large oven capable of baking them. The addition of spices such as nutmeg and cinnamon to the mixture was said to be a tribute to the wise men. The cakes gradually got bigger and more elaborate featuring wonderful sugar decorations and plaster figures. Special scenes were depicted – not the ubiquitous snowman and robin – but huge depictions of sea battles, for example, featuring fully rigged ships and cannons that actually fired!

By the end of the 19th century the original religious significance of Twelfth Night had really been forgotten and it was just an excuse for excessive drinking, eating and mischief making. When only 25 and 26 December were recognised as official bank holidays in 1871, the special Twelfth Night celebrations declined – as did the size of the cake!

THE FAMOUS 18TH-CENTURY PASTRY-COOK-TURNED-ACTOR Robert Baddeley left instructions in his will that a special cake should be given to the cast playing at London's Theatre Royal on Twelfth Night. This has been done nearly every year since 1794 with only wartime restrictions occasionally preventing this popular custom.

BAKERS AND CONFECTIONERS vied with each other to produce the most elaborate Twelfth Night cakes and people would congregate outside their windows to admire the results. It was rather like going up to London to admire the Christmas lights (*see* p 106)! Unfortunately this was a field day for mischievous boys who used to nail the people's clothes to the shop fronts while they were lost in admiration at the cakes displayed!

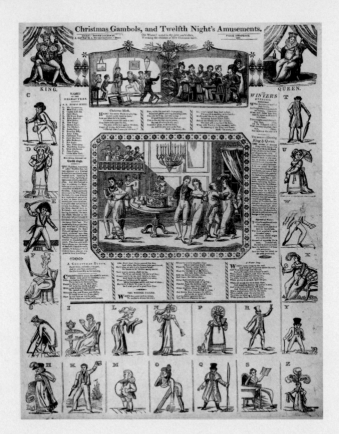

> " THESE WERE MY GUESTS, and Mrs. Turner's friend, whom I saw the other day, Mr. Wicken, and very merry we were at dinner, and so all the afternoon, talking, and looking up and down my house; and in the evening I did bring out my cake – a noble cake, and there cut it into pieces, with wine and good drink: and after a new fashion, to prevent spoiling the cake, did put so many titles into a hat, and so drew cuts; and I was the Queene; and The. Turner, King–Creed, Sir Martin Marr-all; and Betty, Mrs. Millicent: and so we were mighty merry till it was night; and then, being moonshine and fine frost, they went home, I lending some of them my coach to help to carry them, and so my wife and I spent the rest of the evening in talk and reading, and so with great pleasure to bed.
>
> Samuel Pepys, *Diary*, 6 January 1669 "

An early engraving depicting 'Christmas gambols and Twelfth Night amusements'.

Eat, Drink and Be Merry

Christmas Cake

As the tradition of Twelfth Night festivals declined in the late 19th century, the Twelfth Night cake also lost its appeal. However, all the bakers and confectioners who had profited from the sale of these elaborate confections needed a new way to earn an income. So they began producing smaller iced fruit cakes for Christmas parties often decorated with holly leaves, snow scenes etc.

The Christmas cake is traditionally made well in advance and then 'fed' with brandy, whisky or sherry to add to its flavour and richness. Nowadays many people have their own favourite recipes often passed down through the generations. Some prefer the traditional heavy dark cake thick with fruit while others enjoy a lighter textured cake – some people like to add a topping of marzipan and icing while others use nuts or glacé fruits instead. Whatever the style and whether shop bought or homemade, the Christmas cake is still an intrinsic element in Christmas celebrations.

In the 19th century Christmas hampers were sent out to friends and relatives living in Britain's far-flung colonies. These invariably contained a Christmas cake which had been cooked by boiling to ensure it lasted longer.

The flavour of a Christmas fruit cake is enhanced if it is eaten with a hard cheese like Wensleydale or Cheshire.

61

25th (Christmas Day)

"Up pretty early, leaving my wife not well in bed, and with my boy walked, it being a most brave cold and dry frosty morning, and had a pleasant walk to White Hall, where I intended to have received the Communion with the family, but I came a little too late. So I walked up into the house and spent my time looking over pictures, particularly the ships in King Henry the VIIIth's Voyage to Bullen [Boulogne], marking the great difference between their build then and now. By and by down to the chappell again where Bishopp Morley preached upon the song of the Angels, 'Glory to God on high, on earth peace, and good will towards men.' Methought he made but a poor sermon, but long, and reprehending the mistaken jollity of the Court for the true joy that shall and ought to be on these days, he particularized concerning their excess in plays and gaming, saying that he whose office it is to keep the gamesters in order and within bounds, serves but for a second rather in a duell, meaning the groom-porter. Upon which it was worth observing how far they are come from taking the reprehensions of a bishopp seriously, that they all laugh in the chappell when he reflected on their ill actions and courses. He did much press us to joy in these publique days of joy, and to hospitality. But one that stood by whispered in my ear that the Bishopp himself do not spend one groat to the poor himself. The sermon done, a good anthem followed, with vialls, and then the King came down to receive the Sacrament. But I staid not, but calling my boy from my Lord's lodgings, and giving Sarah some good advice, by my Lord's order, to be sober and look after the house, I walked home again with great pleasure, and there dined by my wife's bed-side with great content, having a mess of brave plum-porridge and a roasted pullet for dinner, and I sent for a mince-pie abroad, my wife not being well to make any herself yet. After dinner sat talking a good while with her, her [pain] being become less, and then to see Sir W. Pen a little, and so to my office, practising arithmetique alone and making an end of last night's book with great content till eleven at night, and so home to supper and to bed.

Samuel Pepys, *Diary*, 1662"

OPPOSITE
Pepys' Christmas dinner as depicted at the Geffrye Museum, London.

62

Eat, Drink and Be Merry

Drink

'Twas Christmas broached the mightiest ale;
'Twas Christmas told the merriest tale...

Sir Walter Scott, *Marmion*, 1808

As the natural, and essential, accompaniment
to food, drink at Christmas-time has
traditionally been as rich and lavish as the
meals. Invariably, to add to the festive
feeling, most were, and still are, alcoholic.
From earliest times, ale and wine laced with
seasonal spices were quaffed in honour of
this special time of the year and today most
of us still enjoy our mulled wine and punch.

There have been times when Christmas celebrations were literally more sober – such as during the Commonwealth period (1649–60) when the consumption of alcohol was forbidden, and wartime years when many favourite tipples were difficult to come by. During the Second World War, when alcohol was scarce and expensive, arrests for drunken behaviour at Christmas-time markedly fell. Of course, people still managed to have a good time and probably enjoyed the festive season even more without a sore head!

In the 20th century the Christmas holiday period became a favourite time for the cocktail party, a sophisticated celebration separate from the main Christmas meal. Later this developed into the 'drinks' party with the ubiquitous cheese and pineapple cubes on cocktail sticks. Now there is such a wide range of drinks available to the consumer that we can raise a glass of more or less whatever we want and, with more awareness of the danger

of drinking and then driving, non-alcoholic wines
and cocktails have become increasingly popular too.

Sharing special Christmas drinks – intoxicating
or not – is a key element throughout the history of
Christmas ranging from the wassail bowl to the
office and family parties of modern times. These
traditions and rituals are still just as important as
they have always been and underline the importance
of spreading good will to all. ❄

Wassail

THIS CONVIVIAL CUSTOM is regrettably in decline but it was once a vital element in Christmas and New Year celebrations around the country. Villages would have a large bowl that was kept for the occasion and this would be filled with hot, spiced ale and taken around the households with great ceremony. Drinking from the wassail bowl was said to ensure good luck for the coming year and anyone could enjoy a cup of the wassail in return for food or money.

The name is said to derive from the Old English *Waes hael* meaning 'be well/healthy' – a special toast that may have formed part of the traditional turn-of-year celebrations in a lord's household. Toast (the bread form) also features in some wassail recipes as it was often floated on top of the spiced ale to add to the flavour. It is sometimes claimed that this practice led to the wassail drink being known as 'Lamb's Wool' in some regions, but it is more likely that it was so called because roasted apples (often crab apples) were put in the bowl and these would burst open to reveal their fluffy white insides.

Wassails varied across the country with each area having its own special (and often closely guarded) recipe. In some regions, particularly where cider-making was an important industry, fruit trees were ceremoniously sprinkled with ale or cider from the wassail bowl to ensure a good crop the following year. Villagers carrying pots, pans and sticks would gather around a selected tree and then, at a given signal, bang the pots and pans with the sticks in order to raise the sleeping Tree Spirit and scare off demons by the noise. Pieces of toast were hung in the orchard trees and a special wassail song was sung, with voices no doubt lubricated with the contents of the wassail bowl. This wassail ceremony was

A traditional wassail bowl and cups.

traditionally performed on Twelfth Night although some areas performed it on each of the 12 days of Christmas – which must have resulted in a few headaches!

> Wassail the trees, that they may bear
> You many a plum and many a pear:
> For more or less fruits they will bring
> As you do give them wassailing.
>
> Robert Herrick (1591–1674)

The wassail bowl itself was usually carved from wood – particularly ash. Pottery bowls were also popular and the potter would use his imagination in the design to make it unique. Some bowls were made of precious metal and Jesus College, Oxford, owns a silver wassail bowl that can hold ten gallons. The *Oxford Dictionary* definition of wassail as 'a lot of revelry with drinking' seems particularly apt!

A *Punch* political cartoon from 29 December 1888 showing Father Christmas with a wassail bowl.

WASSAIL SONG

THIS IS REALLY A FORM OF CAROL and wassaillers, carol singers or Waits are all very similar (*see* p 145).

> Here we come a-wassailing
> Among the leaves so green,
> Here we come a-wand'ring
> So fair to be seen.
>
> Love and joy come to you,
> And to you your wassail too
> And God bless you and send you
> A Happy New Year,
> And God send you a Happy New Year.

LAMB'S WOOL

6 apples, cored
3 tbsp brown sugar
4 pints (2.27 litres) cider (or beer)
¼ tsp nutmeg
¼ tsp cinnamon
¼ tsp ground ginger

Roast the apples in a baking tray at 230°C (450°F) for about an hour, or until they are very soft and begin to burst open. Then place in a large punch bowl. Put the cider (or beer) into a large saucepan and gently heat. Stir in the sugar a tablespoon at a time and then add the spices. Bring to a boil and simmer for 10 to 15 minutes. Pour the liquid over the apples and serve.

When icicles hang by the wall
And Dick the shepherd blows his nail
And Tom bears logs into the hall
And milk comes frozen home in pail;
When blood is nipt, and ways be foul,
Then nightly sings the staring owl
Tu-whoo!
Tu-whit! Tu-whoo! A merry note!
While greasy Joan doth keel the pot.

When all around the wind doth blow,
And coughing drowns the parson's saw,
And birds sit brooding in the snow,
And Marian's nose looks red and raw;
When roasted crabs hiss in the bowl –
Then nightly sings the staring owl
Tu-whoo!

William Shakespeare (1564–1616)

71

PIG AND WHISTLE: A pub name that means the wassail-cup and
wassail. A 'pig' is a word for a small cup and 'whistle' is a derivative of
'wassail'.

THE CUSTOM OF WASSAILING was felt to have pagan origins by the
Christian Church but instead of abolishing it they adapted it. The
wassail bowl became the 'loving cup' passed around after grace at
monasteries and other religious houses.

Christmas Cocktails

Shaken or stirred the cocktail adds a certain sophistication to Christmas festivities. Whether served at parties, bars or family gatherings, it can be made from a vast range of alcoholic and non-alcoholic ingredients. Cocktails were originally a mixture of spirits and bitters, although now they can be made from virtually anything.

The origin of the name is obscure and all sorts of weird and wonderful stories have been suggested. Was it from an 18th-century Mexican princess called Coc'tel or could it derive from the English custom of cutting a horse's tail if it wasn't a thoroughbred? Such a horse was known as a 'cock-tail' – just like the one ridden by a lady to Banbury Cross in the nursery rhyme – and its mixed breeding reflected the mixture of ingredients in the drink. Perhaps it derived from 'cock's ale' – a rather revolting sounding mixture of boiled chicken, fruit and spices that was supposedly served during cock-fights. Or did it indeed originate from North America during the War of Independence when some cockerels were reputedly stolen from behind the British lines by American soldiers? The birds were cooked up for them by one Betsy Flanagan who ran a bar in Hall's Corners, New York, and who was famous for her speciality mixed drink called 'Betsy's Bloomers'. The soldiers and some of their French comrades thoroughly enjoyed their meal which was accompanied by copious amounts of 'Betsy's Bloomers'. Feathers left over from the plucked birds were apparently used to decorate the glasses and the Frenchmen toasted her with the words, '*Vive le cock tail!*'

The cocktail became the epitome of sophistication in the 1920s and 1930s when numerous cocktail bars opened offering an incredible variety of exotic-sounding drinks like Singapore Slings, Harvey Wallbangers, Pina Coladas and Tequila Sunrises. The whole experience of drinking cocktails became part of an entertaining evening out and the way they were prepared (with much flourish and a juggling act of cocktail shakers and glasses) was just as much fun as drinking the end product.

In the 1950s cocktail parties were an elegant way to entertain guests at home, with the drinks accompanied by side dishes of carefully prepared hors d'oeuvres and peanuts. Today the cocktail is once again enjoying great popularity and a bewildering array of new combinations with some astonishing names are on offer.

THE NAME 'COCKTAIL' has been in use since at least May 1806 when the intriguingly named American newspaper *The Balance and Columbian Repository* used it in an article about local elections. When a reader wrote in to enquire about the meaning of 'cocktail', the newspaper printed this reply:

Cocktail is a stimulating liquor composed of spirits of any kind, sugar, water, and bitters – it is vulgarly called a bittered sling and is supposed to be an excellent electioneering potion, inasmuch as it renders the heart stout and bold, at the same time that it fuddles the head. It is said also to be of great use to a Democratic candidate: because a person, having swallowed a glass of it, is ready to swallow anything else.

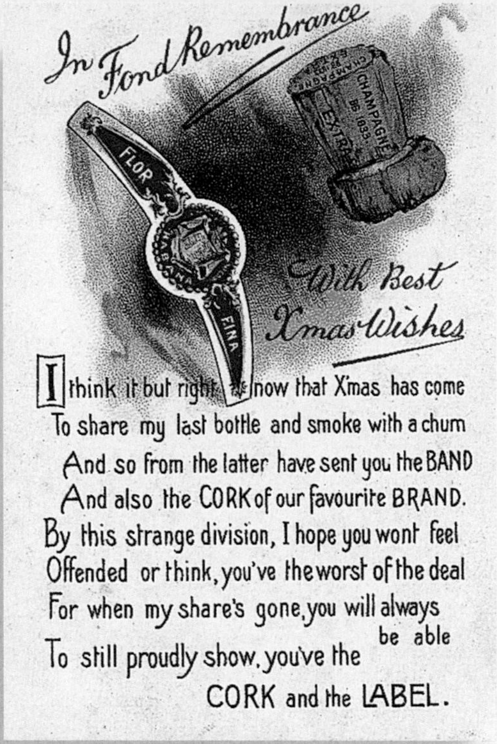

In Fond Remembrance

With Best Xmas Wishes

I think it but right, now that Xmas has come
To share my last bottle and smoke with a chum
And so from the latter have sent you the BAND
And also the CORK of our favourite BRAND.
By this strange division, I hope you wont feel
Offended or think, you've the worst of the deal
For when my share's gone, you will always be able
To still proudly show, you've the
CORK and the LABEL.

CHAMPAGNE COCKTAIL

Angostura bitters
1 sugar cube
Cognac
Champagne

Put about 4 dashes of the bitters on a sugar cube and place in the bottom of a champagne flute. Cover the cube with cognac – then top up with champagne.

―――――――

" THE COCKTAIL PARTY is a device for paying off obligations to people you don't want to invite for dinner. "
Anon

Mulled Wine

THIS FESTIVE DRINK is perfect to offer chilly carol singers or soothe fraught Mums trying to wrap parcels, stuff turkeys and bake mince pies all at the same time! The delicious smell of cloves, nutmeg and cinnamon is almost as heady as the effect of the drink itself!

As well as being delicious it has long been thought that mulled wine is good for you; it was often given as a health drink or tonic. It is claimed that the 'mull' was a 17th-century verb meaning 'to stupefy'!

MULLED WINE

1 bottle of fruity red wine

10–12 cloves

1 orange

4 tbsp soft brown sugar

Rind of one lemon

1 stick cinnamon

Freshly ground nutmeg to taste

2 bay leaves

½ pint (275 ml) brandy (optional)

Pour the wine into a saucepan with a heavy base. Stick cloves into the orange and then place it in the pan along with the rest of the ingredients (except the brandy if you are using that). Heat until nearly boiling, then add the brandy and heat until really hot. Serve in previously warmed glasses.

There are lots of different ways of mulling wine and it is really trial and error until you find the flavour that suits you. If you want a sweeter drink add more sugar or honey and if you want it spicier increase the amount of cinnamon or try a bit of ground ginger. Many people add apple juice to reduce the alcoholic potency while others pep it up even more by adding a fruity liquor like sloe gin or Gran Marnier – the possibilities are almost endless! You can even buy mulled wine bags rather like teabags which you simply add to the hot wine. And you don't even have to use wine – try mulling cider or fruit juice instead.

———————

GLÜHWEIN is a type of mulled wine particularly popular at Christmas in Germany, Austria and Switzerland. It translates very appropriately as 'glowing wine'! It is traditionally served with iced ginger biscuits.

———————

THE SPICES USUALLY USED for mulled wine are cloves, grated nutmeg, and cinnamon or mace. Any kind of wine may be mulled, but port and claret are those usually selected for the purpose.

Mrs Isabella Beeton, *Book of Household Management*, 1838

Grogs, Nogs and Possets

THESE ALCOHOLIC DRINKS are often now enjoyed at Christmas but in previous centuries they were drunk throughout the year – usually on the excuse that they were health-giving tonics.

GROG

A SPIRIT DILUTED WITH WATER. Named after 'Old Grog', the nickname of Admiral Edward Vernon (1684–1757) who was well known for his habit of wearing coats made from grogram (grosgrain) – a coarse, hard-wearing fabric made from a mixture of silk and mohair. Vernon suggested that the Royal Navy's daily rum ration should be diluted with 50 per cent water to reduce drunkenness and when this was quickly introduced the ration became known as a 'grog'. We still use the term 'groggy' to mean weak or unsteady.

BUT EVEN HERE, two men who watched the light had made a fire, that through the loophole in the thick stone wall shed out a ray of brightness on the awful sea. Joining their horny hands over the rough table at which they sat, they wished each other Merry Christmas in their can of grog; and one of them: the elder, too, with his face all damaged and scarred with hard weather, as the figure-head of an old ship might be: struck up a sturdy song that was like a Gale in itself.

Charles Dickens, *A Christmas Carol*, 1843

NOG

A SPIRIT-BASED DRINK which includes milk and eggs and is very similar to a posset. It is a traditional pick-me-up and egg nog is very popular in the USA. Carved wooden mugs used to be known as 'noggins' and a 'noggin' is also a small measure of alcohol of about ¼ pint (142 ml).

THE FRENCHMAN SOON JOINED THE GERMAN and the sheriff in the hall, who compelled him to take a seat with them at the table, where, by the aid of punch, wine, and egg nog, they soon extracted from the complaisant Monsieur Le Quoi the nature of his visit, it was evident that he had made the offer, as a duty which a well-bred man owed to a lady in such a retired place, before he had left the country, and that his feelings were but very little, if at all, interested in the matter.

James Fenimore Cooper, *The Pioneers*, 1868

EGG NOG

6 eggs
6 oz (170 g) caster sugar
4 fl oz (110 ml) rum
12 fl oz (340 ml) brandy
1½ pints (850 ml) milk
1½ pints (850 ml) cream
4 oz (110 g) icing sugar
Ground nutmeg to taste

Separate the eggs. Slowly beat the sugar into the egg yolks until pale gold. Slowly add the rum and brandy, then beat in the milk and half the cream. Whisk the egg whites until stiff and fold in. Divide into glasses. Whip up the remaining cream with the icing sugar and place on top of each glass. Sprinkle liberally with ground nutmeg before serving.

POSSET

SOOTHING AND SATISFYING, possets are a combination of hot milk/cream and alcohol (sherry or ale) which separates into three distinct layers: at the top is a foam known as the 'grace', below that is a custard-like mixture and at the bottom is the best bit of all – a rich alcoholic liquid.

A special posset cup was traditionally used for this delicacy – it had two handles and a spout in the side which allowed the alcoholic liquid to be sucked out while the first two layers were eaten with a spoon. Like the wassail bowl, the cup was often large enough for it to be passed around for a number of people to take a swig.

Possets were popular in wealthy households from the Middle Ages and were often used to ease aches, pains, coughs and colds, as well as just for pure pleasure. By the 16th and 17th centuries everyone seems to have enjoyed possets – the rich making theirs from sack (the old word for sherry which derived from the French word *sec* meaning dry) and expensive spices, while the poor used ale with some bread thrown in for extra body. An ale posset was traditionally drunk before retiring on Christmas Eve.

Unfortunately, posset making then went into decline and now the only survival is the traditional 'Bride's cog', which is ceremoniously passed among the guests at weddings in the Orkney isles. This hot and heady concoction is a combination of cream, whisky, ale and oatcakes. Delicious!

―――――――――

THIS 17TH-CENTURY RECIPE is entitled 'a posset' but it is really more of a nog. It was recorded by Sir Kenelm Digby (1603–65) after it was given to him by Charles Howard, 1st Earl of Carlisle. Sir Kenelm was an important courtier, naval commander and diplomat who Charles I sent to ask for the Pope's help in the English Civil War. He was also a skilled scientist and an early member of the Royal Society. However, he was quite eccentric and became renowned for inventing 'sympathetic' powder, an astonishing concoction which was supposed to cure wounds – not by being put on the injuries but on the weapons which had inflicted them! His wife, Lady Venetia Stanley, died in 1635 after reputedly drinking 'viper wine' to keep her complexion beautiful – whether this was on the advice of her husband is not known.

MY LORD OF CARLISLE'S SACK POSSET

Take a Pottle of Cream, and boil in it a little whole Cinnamon, and three or four flakes of Mace. To this proportion of Cream put in eighteen yolkes of Eggs, and eight of the whites; a pint of Sack. Beat your eggs very well, and mingle them with your Sack. Put in three quarters of a pound of Sugar into the Wine and Eggs with a Nutmeg grated, and a little beaten Cinnamon; set the basin on the fire with the wine and Eggs, and let it be hot. Then put in the Cream boyling from the fire, pour it on high, but stir it not; cover it with a dish, and when it is settled, strew on the top a little fine sugar mingled with three grains of Ambergreece and one grain of Musk and serve it up.

Sir Kenelm Digby, *The Closet of Sir Kenelm Digby Knight Opened*, 1669

A tin-glazed earthenware posset bowl and stand made in Bristol in 1685.

THE MODERN EQUIVALENT OF THIS RECIPE IS:

9 egg yolks

4 egg whites

½ pint (275 ml) dry sherry

¼ tsp cinnamon

¼ tsp ground mace

½ tsp grated nutmeg

2 pints (1.1 litres) single cream

6 oz (175 g) sugar

Beat together the egg yolks, egg whites, sherry and spices. Place in a large saucepan and heat gently, stirring constantly until warm but still not thickened. Heat the cream and sugar together in a pan and, as the liquid rises to the full boil, pour from a good height into the warm eggs and sherry mixture. Allow the posset to stand in a warm place for a few minutes, then sprinkle a little sugar across the top and serve.

———————

TRADITIONAL RECIPE FOR ALE POSSET

Place a quart of strong ale or beer in a large bowl, grate in a little nutmeg, and sweeten with sugar. Milk the cow rapidly into the bowl, forcing the milk as strongly as possible into the ale and against the sides of the vessel to raise a good froth. Let it stand an hour, and it will be fit for use. The proportion of milk or of sugar will depend on the taste of the drinker who will, after a trial or two, be able to make a delightful beverage. Cider may be used instead of malt liquor, or a bottle of wine.

———————

THE 3RD GLASS.   4th .....   5th .....   6th ......   7th ....   8th 9th

JONES' GLASS HAS BEEN STEADILY FALLING.
(*A Christmas Story in Seven Chapters.*)
Eventually Jones was found under the table, snoring loudly, and with his head in the spitoon.

82

Punch

A FESTIVE COMBINATION of spirits and fruit juice which, like mulled wine and wassail, is traditionally served in a large bowl. It can be far more potent than many other Christmas drinks but nowadays many non-alcoholic punches are popular. The name comes from the Indian *punj* meaning five, and reflects that a punch should have five ingredients – spirits, water, lemon, sugar and spice.

PUNCH … is called 'Contradiction', because it is composed of spirits to make it strong, and water to make it weak; of lemon-juice to make it sour, and sugar to make it sweet.

Brewer's Dictionary of Phrase and Fable, 1898

...Ye Scots, wha wish auld Scotland well!
Ye chief, to you my tale I tell,
Poor, plackless devils like mysel'!
      It sets you ill,
Wi' bitter, dearthfu' wines to mell,
      Or foreign gill.

May gravels round his blather wrench,
An' gouts torment him, inch by inch,
What twists his gruntle wi' a glunch
O' sour disdain,
Out owre a glass o' whisky-punch
      Wi' honest men!

Robert Burns, from *Scotch Drink*, 1785

CHRISTMAS CAROL PUNCH

Dissolve a quarter of a pound of sugar in a pint of boiling water, and pour into a China bowl, which may be one decorated with some formal or pleasing pattern, as fancy may dictate, or piety direct. Add the juice of two lemons, with the rinds, half a pint of ginger brandy, one bottle of Jamaica rum, a few sticks of cinnamon, a handful of cloves, and six orange slices. Allow to simmer, and serve hot in punch glasses. A silver ladle is customary.

Recipe by H McElhone, quoted in *A Christmas Book*, 1928

...This ancient silver bowl of mine,—it tells of good old times
Of joyous days, and jolly nights, and merry Christmas chimes,
They were a free and jovial race, but honest, brave, and true,
That dipped their ladle in the punch when this old bowl was new.

Oliver Wendell Holmes, from *On Lending a Punch-bowl* (1809–94)

Non-Alcoholic

CHILDREN HAVE LONG BEEN ALLOWED special drinks at Christmas – sometimes a little of what the adults were enjoying but more often special non-alcoholic cocktails or fizzy drinks. Increasingly, adults are realising that Christmas is more fun if Boxing Day isn't spent recovering from a hangover and the importance of not drinking alcohol and driving has made more and more people choose non-alcoholic beverages to celebrate with.

PLAIN WATER IS DECIDEDLY BEST... Many children will drink water, or a little sherry and water; but for moderately sized children, who do not care to take water, what can be better than home-made lemonade? To my thinking a glass of lemonade is far preferable to cheap champagne, and far less vulgar. Why poison your guests for the sake of appearances?

Cassell's Family Magazine

HOME-MADE LEMONADE

6 large unwaxed lemons
5 oz (150 g) granulated sugar
4½ pints (2½ litres) water (boiling)

Wash the lemons and grate off the zest. Squeeze out the juice into a large bowl, add the grated zest and sugar and then carefully pour on the boiling water. Cover and leave to cool. Keep for 24 hours stirring occasionally and adding extra sugar if not sweet enough. Strain through a sieve and pour into sterilised bottles. Serve straight or add to sparkling water.

Be Merry

...Then came the merry masquers in,
And carols roared with blithesome din
If unmelodious was the song,
It was a hearty note, and strong.
Who lists may in their mumming see
Traces of ancient mystery;
White shirts supplied the masquerade,
And smutted cheeks the visors made;
But, oh! what masquers, richly dight,
Can boast of bosoms half so light!
England was merry England, when
Old Christmas brought his sports again,
... A Christmas gambol oft could cheer
The poor man's heart through half the year.

Sir Walter Scott, *Marmion*, 1808

Sir Walter Scott's lines beautifully sum up the idea of Christmas as a time for celebrating and 'making merry'. Decorating the house, setting out the Christmas crackers, exchanging gifts and cards and anticipating Santa's visit – all contribute to the festivities. Games, theatrical productions and other entertainments have long been popular too. And today popular Christmas entertainment in film and on television and radio has become part of our modern tradition.

The Church makes merry as well with peals of bells, carol singing and special services all encouraging a feeling of joy about the true meaning of Christmas. ❄

88

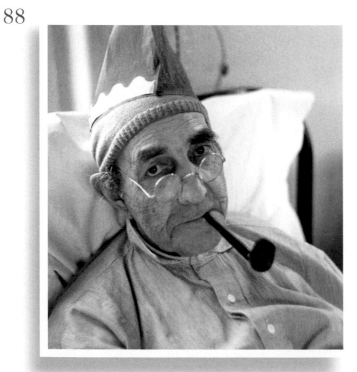

Decorating

CHRISTMAS COMES WITH A LONG TRADITION of holiday rituals, some of which are now rather rare. But one of the most popular and merry of Christmas traditions is the tree.

O CHRISTMAS TREE!

O Christmas Tree! O Christmas Tree!
Thy candles shine so brightly!
O Christmas Tree! O Christmas Tree!
Thy candles shine so brightly!
From base to summit, gay and bright,
There's only splendour for the sight.
O Christmas Tree! O Christmas Tree!
Thy candles shine so brightly!

Traditional German carol

WHAT COULD BE MORE FESTIVE on a dark snowy night than the twinkling lights of a Christmas tree shining out of a house window? Christmas trees are a German tradition going back to at least the 16th century, though there is some speculation that precursors can be found in the Paradise Tree or Tree of Life seen in medieval mystery plays about Adam and Eve, and also in the use of evergreens in earlier pagan celebrations. The custom seems to have first come to Britain with Queen Charlotte, the German wife of George III, who arranged for a Christmas tree to be set up for the royal family during the 1780s and 1790s. But it wasn't until the reign of Queen Victoria that the Christmas tree became popular – indeed, Prince Albert has often been credited with its introduction to a wider audience as the public clamoured to copy the royal family's new Christmas tradition. Victoria and Albert had a decorated tree on display at Windsor and Osborne House in the years after their marriage in 1840 – in one of her diary entries Victoria wrote: 'Today I have two children of my own to give presents

to who, they know not why, are full of happy wonder at the German Christmas tree and its radiant candles.' And in 1848 the *Illustrated London News* showed an engraving of the happy family gathered round their Christmas tree at Windsor.

Initially Christmas trees were relatively small and placed in pots on tabletops, rather than set up in a base on the floor. The gifts were displayed round the foot of the tree unwrapped, or were hung from the branches as additional decorations. Larger trees became more common from the 1880s when an English-grown species, the Norway Spruce, began to replace the smaller German Springelbaum. The first artificial trees were seen in Britain by 1860 – for example trees made of goose feathers (often dyed green) were decorated with small ornaments and displayed on tabletops and in windows, and during the Edwardian period Christmas trees were sometimes made from coloured ostrich feathers. More naturalistic artificial trees later developed, but there has always been a taste for the more unusual, which now includes metallic or coloured trees, trees made with fibre optic lights, coloured trees, trees dusted with fake snow and even ones that sing Christmas carols!

Early decorations were handmade and simple, including paper flowers, gilded and plain fruits and nuts, wax candles, sugar candies and gingerbread. More elaborate ornaments – and ones made specifically for the Christmas market – developed as the popularity of Christmas trees grew. In the 19th century the specialised manufacture of Christmas tree decorations developed in Germany, especially with the blown glass ornaments that grew out of the already established glass industry in Lauscha, Thuringia. The earliest designs were of fruit and pine cones and by 1870 the artisans had developed a silvering

technique to line the inside of the ornaments so they would reflect the lights. F W Woolworth stumbled upon Lauscha's glass ornament industry in the 1890s and soon saw the potential market for their beautiful decorations. He began buying the ornaments for his stores, where they quickly became very popular. In 1909 alone he bought around 216,000 glass baubles! Other types of tree decoration included patriotic flags, which were particularly fashionable during the Crimean War. And while candles continued to be used, there were obvious fire hazards in the use of lit tapers on live – and artificial – Christmas trees. The American inventor Edward H Johnson, known as the Father of Electric Christmas Tree Lights, solved the problem when he had a strand of coloured incandescent bulbs made for his own Christmas tree in 1882. While at first electric lights were an expensive luxury, they had become fairly widespread by the late 1930s. Today tinsel is also a popular tree decoration and the tree is usually crowned by a star, angel or fairy.

92

OSLO, NORWAY HAS GIVEN A SPRUCE TREE to Britain every year since 1947 to commemorate the British support they received during the Second World War. This tree is displayed in Trafalgar Square in London after a lighting ceremony (*see* left).

TRADITIONALLY, the Christmas tree should be decorated on Christmas Eve and taken down on 6 January. It is considered bad luck to leave the tree up and decorated past this date.

DECK THE HALLS WITH BOUGHS OF HOLLY...

EVERGREEN AND HOLLY WREATHS hanging on front doors, garlands of greenery festooning candle-lit mantelpieces and the tops of windows and doors, table centrepieces of shiny red apples, pine cones and fragrant pine and fir branches – all are popular adornments to our houses at Christmas-time. Decorating in this fashion is another custom born in the pagan past when evergreens – such as holly, ivy, bay, laurel and rosemary – were commonly displayed and exchanged during the various midwinter festivals. For example the Romans exchanged sprigs of greenery during the Saturnalia and adorned their houses and temples with evergreens. Decorating with greenery during the pre-Christian period was seen as a way to bring about good luck and fertility at this bleak time of the year and also as a symbol of everlasting life as these plants continue to grow and bloom during the winter. It was also believed that by bringing greenery into your house you would provide a warm refuge for the sylvan spirits, who would reward your kindness with luck and prosperity in the coming year. Though some people in the early church questioned the practice of decorating with evergreens because of their association with earlier pagan practices, it was later embraced as a Christian symbol of everlasting life and a way to mark the Christmas holiday and bring a festive air to the proceedings. And supposedly Pope Gregory endorsed the practice in Britain during the 7th century as a way of encouraging the followers of the old pagan religions to more easily accept Christianity.

Christianity and the Christmas tree

There are two stories relating the Christmas tree to Christian tradition. The legend of St Boniface tells us that he felled an oak sacred to Thor, the god of thunder, and built a chapel from its timber in AD 723. The pagan Germanic tribes in the area were converted to Christianity when they saw that their god did not strike him down for this sacrilegious act. He then used the triangular shape of a fir tree, which grew in place of the oak, to explain the concept of the Holy Trinity to the newly Christianised Germans.

The Christmas tree is also associated with the German religious reformer Martin Luther. Supposedly he was walking in the woods one Christmas Eve when he was moved by the beauty of the starry sky. He is said to have brought a fir tree back to his house, where he decorated it with candles, saying that the evergreen represented God's creation and Jesus's birth while the candles symbolised the stars he saw shining brightly on that cold winter night. He also crowned the tree with a candle to represent the Star of Bethlehem.

In fact, the church gave Christian symbolism to some of the greenery traditionally seen in pre-Christian festivities. Despite its early use in pagan customs and its association with protection from evil spirits, holly was made into a Christian symbol when its prickly leaves were likened to Christ's crown of thorns and its red berries to the shedding of Christ's blood for human salvation; in Denmark holly is actually called the Christ-thorn.

94

As with the Christmas tree, there was a superstition about when all the Christmas greenery should be taken down – it was believed that the greenery should remain on display until Candlemas (2 February), the traditional end of winter, and for every piece of greenery that was accidentally left in the house after that date, a goblin would haunt the house! The 17th-century poet Robert Herrick expressed this view in his poem *Ceremony upon Candlemas Eve*:

> Down with the rosemary, and so
> Down with the bays and misletoe;
> Down with the holly, ivy, all
> Wherewith ye dress'd the Christmas hall;
> That so the superstitious find
> No one least branch there left behind;
> For look, how many leaves there be
> Neglected there, maids, trust to me,
> So many goblins you shall see.

Over-decked with Greens...

In a late 17th/early 18th-century letter to the *Spectator*, a woman called Jenny Simper wrote:

I am a young Woman and have my Fortune to make, for which Reason I come constantly to Church to hear divine Service and make Conquests; but one great Hindrance in this my Design is, that our Clerk, who was once a Gardener, has this Christmas so over-decked the Church with Greens, that he has quite spoil'd my

Prospect, inasmuch that I have scarce seen the young Baronet I dress at these three Weeks, though we have both been very Constant at our Devotions, and do not sit above three Pews off...The middle Isle is a very pretty Shady Walk, and the Pews look like so many Arbours on each Side of it. The Pulpit itself has such Clusters of Ivy, Holly, and Rosemary about it, that a light Fellow in our Pew took Occasion to say, that the Congregation heard the Word out of a Bush, like Moses.

She goes on to ask the *Spectator* to 'give Orders for removing these Greens' so she doesn't grow into a very awkward creature who only comes to church for prayers!

The accused Clerk writes to the *Spectator* the next day, stating that he hasn't done this because he used to be a gardener but to spite Miss Simper — and other ladies like her — and to prevent her from making any conquests at all!

MISTLETOE AND THE KISSING BOUGH

I saw Mama kissing Santa Claus
Underneath the mistletoe last night...

(Christmas song recorded by Jimmy Boyd in 1952)

IN THE PREHISTORIC PAST mistletoe – a parasitic plant that grows on the branches of trees and shrubs – was reputedly venerated by the Druids and was an important part of their religious rituals, especially those that took place around the winter solstice. Along with its medicinal uses, it was believed to have protective properties, bring good luck and ensure fertility. It is believed that for many years it was not included in the greenery used to decorate churches at Christmas because of its association with the pagan past. Washington Irving highlights this belief in his book *Old Christmas* (1876):

MARIE: "If you don't behave better, Miss Maudie, I shall tell the mistress about you insulting my father!"
MISS MAUDIE: "Do, and I'll tell her about you kissing mine under the mistletoe!"
No. 612—Old Series.

On reaching the church-porch, we found the parson rebuking the grey-headed sexton for having used the mistletoe among the greens with which the church was decorated. It was, he observed, an unholy plant, profaned by having been used by the Druids in their mystic ceremonies; and though it might be innocently employed in the festive ornamenting of halls and kitchens, yet it had been deemed by the Fathers of the Church as unhallowed, and totally unfit for sacred purposes. So tenacious was he on this point, that the poor sexton was obliged to strip down a great part of the humble trophies of his taste, before the parson would consent to enter upon the service of the day.

There is a legend that the mistletoe was once a tree and that its wood was used to make Christ's cross – afterwards the mistletoe was so ashamed that it changed from a tree into a creeper! Perhaps this story is another reason why mistletoe was sometimes kept out of the evergreen decorations placed in churches.

These concerns seem very far from the associations of mistletoe today, where it primarily evokes the thrill of kisses stolen underneath its sprigs hung from rafters and door frames at Christmas-time. The significance of mistletoe in matters of the heart is a long-standing one, with its origins as an emblem of love going back to Scandinavian mythology and the tale of Baldur. Baldur, the son of Odin, dreamed of his own death – fearing that this was a prophetic dream, his mother Frigga made every living or growing thing on earth promise never to harm him. Unfortunately, the small and seemingly insignificant mistletoe was not included in this vow. Because Baldur was now believed to be indestructible, one of the gods' favourite pastimes was to throw all manner of things at him to try to kill him as he remained unscathed. However, Loki, the god of mischief, made a small arrow out of mistletoe wood and tricked the blind god Hod into throwing the weapon at Baldur, who was killed by it. After a long period of mourning, Baldur was eventually resurrected by the other gods and Frigga declared that from then on mistletoe would be a plant associated with love rather than death. Another legend says that the white mistletoe berries were the tears Frigga shed at her son's death.

And once again, superstitions have arisen around mistletoe – for example it was believed that if a girl does not get kissed beneath the mistletoe at Christmas, she will not marry during the following year. Because of this, mistletoe was often hung where it was impossible to avoid, thus lessening the chance of being a loser in matters of the heart! Another custom is for the man to remove a berry from the mistletoe each time he kisses a girl beneath it; once all the berries are gone the mistletoe can no longer be used for romantic trysts.

Mistletoe and other greenery were often arranged into a ring or a round ball originally called a Holy Bough and later a 'kissing bough'. Hung from the ceiling, the wooden hoop or sphere was adorned with fir-cones, fruit, ears of corn or oats, dolls, candles, coloured paper, ribbons and sometimes an effigy of Christ or the Holy Family. This English custom appears to pre-date the use of mistletoe on its own and goes back to the 15th century; as with the mistletoe it was also meant to encourage embraces (supposedly representing goodwill) beneath its boughs, though this aspect of the tradition does not seem to have become truly established until the 18th century.

A Tudor-style kissing bough decorated with greenery and fruit.

YULE LOG

Come bring with a noise,
My merry, merry boys,
      The Christmas-log to the firing;
While my good dame she
Bids ye all be free,
      And drink to your heart's desiring.

With the last year's brand
Light the new block, and,
      For good success in his spending,
On your psalteries play
That sweet luck may
      Come while the log is a tending…

Robert Herrick, *Christmas Ceremonies*, c 1630

The Yule Log was originally a Scandinavian tradition set around the feast of Juul (the winter solstice) when bonfires were built in honour of Odin, the chief god of Norse mythology; it was later embraced as a Christmas custom in England. Amongst great ceremony, the new Yule Log – sometimes an entire tree, which would stick out from the hearth into the room – would be brought into the house on Christmas Eve. It was decorated with greenery and ribbons and lit from the remnants of the previous year's log. In order to guarantee good luck for the coming year, the log had to be kept continuously burning for the 12 days of Christmas (though some sources claim just 12 hours). If a tree had been used, this meant feeding it into the hearth throughout the 12 days as it slowly burned down. Other superstitions – like the idea that it provided protection from witches, misfortune and, ironically, house fire – arose around the burning of the Yule Log. It was also

considered bad luck if a squinting person, a bare-footed person or a flat-footed woman entered the room when the log was burning – that must have precluded a lot of the general population from joining in the festivities!

———————

THERE IS A FRENCH CHOCOLATE CAKE made at Christmas in the shape of the Yule Log called the *Bûche de Noël*. In some places in France, the Yule log tradition is also followed, though with the added embellishment of sprinkling the log with wine so that it gives off an enticing smell as it burns!

———————

CHRISTMAS CRACKERS

THE CHRISTMAS CRACKER was invented in 1847 by Tom Smith, a London confectioner. He based the idea on French bon-bons – sugared almonds and sweets that were twisted up in coloured tissue paper.

At first crackers did not really catch on with the general public, despite early gimmicks like the mottoes, poems and love messages that were placed inside the cracker with the sweets. Later, inspired by his crackling log fire, Smith added a saltpetre strip to the design which made a loud 'crack' when the ends were pulled. They were originally called 'cosaques' because the noise they made was said to sound like the crack of a Cossack's whip! As their popularity increased, the sweets were replaced by novelty gifts, a paper hat and a silly joke or riddle, and it became traditional to decorate the Christmas table with the colourful crackers, which were then pulled at the beginning or end of the meal.

While the main market was for the ordinary table-top crackers, Smith also produced special versions, such as his 1905 'Golden Sheaf' cracker, which contained a gold ring set with pearls and cost £400. And one year, for every performance of the Christmas pantomime at Drury Lane, he created a 7ft long cracker that contained a change of costume for the two performers who pulled its ends and a supply of normal-sized crackers to be thrown out into the audience.

THE LARGEST CHRISTMAS CRACKER in the world at the time was made in 2001 by the children of Ley Hill School in Buckinghamshire to raise money for the school and charity. It was 207ft in length and over 13ft wide! It took four days to construct and inside there were 400 balloons, presents for the children, a huge party hat and a joke: 'Why does Father Christmas always look sad? Because he's got the sack!'

SOME CLASSIC CHRISTMAS CRACKER JOKES:

What did the fish say when it swam into a wall?
Dam.

Why are chocolate buttons rude?
Because they are Smarties in the nude.

What sits at the bottom of the sea
and shakes?
A nervous wreck.

What did the grape say when the
elephant stepped on it?
Nothing. It just let out a little wine.

What's ET short for?
Because he's only got little legs.

Punch's Christmas crackers

The popular satirical magazine *Punch* listed out the imagined contents of the crackers of various political figures in its 24 December 1887 issue. These included a 'brand-new map of the Balkan States with Prince Bismarck's compliments' for the Russian Czar; 'a satisfactory explanation of recent Russian Military movements with the Czar's kindest regards' for the Emperor of Austria; and 'German Security by arrangement, with the seasonable wishes from the Five Great Powers' for Prince Bismarck!

CHRISTMAS LIGHT DISPLAYS AND SHOP WINDOWS

MANY PEOPLE FESTOON the outside as well as the inside of their houses with Christmas decorations. Some are simply decorated with coloured or white Christmas lights hung from the eaves of the house, along the roof line and around windows and doors. However, in recent years, the trend for more excessive displays has been gaining momentum, with some houses covered in thousands of lights and front gardens populated with inflatable and plastic Christmas characters. For many families, checking out their neighbours' Christmas lights has become a new Christmas custom. Huge light displays have become so common in the USA that viewing the lights has become an annual tradition in some places – in Richmond, Virginia, this has developed into the 'Tacky Xmas Decoration Contest and Grand Highly Illuminated House Tour', which began in 1986.

SWAROVSKI

The commercial sector has also wholeheartedly embraced the tradition of Christmas displays. Illuminated decorations on city streets began in the 1950s and many people made special trips up to London to see the Christmas lights on Oxford and Regent Streets. Today most towns grace their high streets with lights and other Christmas decorations, often holding special ceremonies for their first lighting, and many shops go to town on their special Christmas window displays. In London many of the large department stores like Liberty, Harrods and Harvey Nichols are well known for their elaborate and creative displays.

———————

Cards and Presents

Christmas cards

Before the advent of Christmas cards, people sent letters to family and friends over the Christmas period and children often prepared little pieces of text for the family as a Christmas sampler of their handwriting. But speciality Christmas cards are essentially an English invention of the Victorian period. In 1843 the first commercial Christmas cards were created by Sir Henry Cole, later the first director of the South Kensington Museum (which became the Victoria & Albert Museum), in order to deal with his overwhelming holiday correspondence and remove the stress of writing to each person individually. The hand-coloured lithograph cards were designed by John Callcott Horsley and bore the greeting 'A Merry Christmas and a Happy New Year to You' along with a central image of a family having their Christmas dinner and scenes of Christmas charity on either side. Cole had around 1,000 of these cards produced and sold those remaining for one shilling each, but because of their high price the

108

cards weren't commercially successful. By the 1860s other companies began producing cheaper Christmas cards and they became more popular, especially with the upper and middle classes. The cheap postal rate (the half-penny post) for postcards and unsealed envelopes in 1870 led to an increase in the number of cards being sent as the practice became more accessible to the masses, which in turn led to the further development of the Christmas card industry.

109

While early Christmas cards could be quite lavish and some were even illustrated by famous artists of the day, the majority were cheap lithographs and were often simply in the form of a postcard. Taking inspiration from the Valentine's Day cards that were already common, they carried a variety of designs, many with little obvious connection to Christmas such as spring flowers, cupids, bows, a variety of animals and even nudes by the seaside! A short article in the December 1900 issue of *The Fireside* even complained about the way many Christmas cards bore no imagery of Christmas.

Today the Christmas card industry is huge. Many Christmas card sales also benefit a variety of charities, and in this increasingly environmentally conscious age, it is becoming common for people to send electronic Christmas cards selected from the multitude of free e-cards available on the internet. Some people also take the opportunity to send out 'round robins' – newsletters that summarise the family's achievements and events during the year – a custom appreciated by some and maligned by many. John Betjeman sums up the Christmas card season well in his poem *Advent* from 1955:

> And how, in fact, do we prepare
> The great day that waits us there –
> For the twenty-fifth day of December,
> The birth of Christ? For some it means
> An interchange of hunting scenes
> On coloured cards, And I remember
> Last year I sent out twenty yards,
> Laid end to end, of Christmas cards
> To people that I scarcely know –
> They'd sent a card to me, and so
> I had to send one back. Oh dear!
> Is this a form of Christmas cheer?
> Or is it, which is less surprising,
> My pride gone in for advertising?
> The only cards that really count
> Are that extremely small amount
> From real friends who keep in touch
> And are not rich but love us much...

CHRISTMAS ENVELOPES – used to send letters during the holidays – existed before Christmas cards. Richard Doyle designed a Christmas envelope in 1840, which was decorated with a picture of Harlequin eating a plum pudding with children and their toys arranged around him.

CHRISTMAS CARDS AND LETTERS are equally popular in the USA. In the early 19th century the Washington, DC postmaster actually wanted

ABOVE
This Victorian advertisement illustrates that commercialism is nothing new at Christmas-time.

110

a law passed to limit the number of cards that each person could send, due to the difficulty of dealing with the enormous amount of mail that went out during the holiday season!

Gift-giving

GIVING AND RECEIVING PRESENTS has long been a core part of Christmas festivities and was also important in some of the earlier pagan celebrations such as the Saturnalia. Once Christmas was established, the theological concept of God giving Jesus to humanity as a gift was embraced. Exchanging presents was also related to the three gifts given to Jesus by the wise men and was seen as a continuance of this idea. Indeed, it became common for English monarchs to actually give gold, frankincense and myrrh as Epiphany gifts, often personally presenting these offerings in the Chapel Royal at St James's Palace.

In general, before the early 19th century, while gift-giving occurred at Christmas, it was primarily a New Year's tradition – for instance, in a diary entry of 1669, Samuel Pepys records that he gave his wife an expensive walnut cabinet as a New Year's Day gift. During the medieval period and also in later centuries, gifts of produce such as apples or eggs were commonly given by the peasant tenants to their landlords, and the landlords often provided a feast in return. During the Tudor and Stuart periods, gifts such as sweets, food, jewellery and scented pomanders were also given to patrons and other 'superiors'. And it wasn't unusual for a monarch to actually specify what sort of present they expected. Sometimes it would be a specific amount

111

of money but other popular presents included leather gloves (for one Christmas alone, Charles I received around 70 pairs).

But it was during the Victorian and Edwardian periods that Christmas gift-giving – and the resulting commercialism – really took off with a particular focus on children. Stores produced huge Christmas catalogues full of gift ideas and holiday advertising appeared in the magazines and newspapers of the day. Common children's presents included toy soldiers, train sets, military uniforms, skipping ropes, books, dolls and prams, Noah's ark sets, rocking horses, dolls' houses, building sets and board games. And, of course, the teddy bear, a perennial favourite!

Today Christmas consumerism is big business and it seems like the holiday advertising begins earlier each year, with TV commercials urging us into the shops and the piped Christmas music and festive decorations appearing on the high streets as early as September. A great deal of criticism has been levelled at this over-commercialism of Christmas – and the stress related to it – with many feeling that the 'reason for the season' is lost in the detritus of wrapping paper and empty boxes left under the tree on Christmas morning. More and more people are deciding to buy ethical gifts that help those less privileged – such as livestock, textbooks and school equipment, tree planting, safe drinking water and basic facilities – through various charitable organisations which provide presents that benefit local people, the global environment and communities in the developing world. 'Buy Nothing Christmas' is another reaction to the commercialisation of the holiday. This movement, started by a group of Canadian Mennonites in 2001, encourages people to de-commercialise Christmas by buying less – and also buying responsibly – and instead focusing on the holiday's original meaning and important aspects of Christmas like spending time with family and friends.

———

We raise the price of things in shops,
We give plain boxes fancy tops
And lines which traders cannot sell
Thus parcell'd go extremely well
We dole out bribes we call a present
To those to whom we must be pleasant
For business reasons. Our defence is
These bribes are charged against expenses
And bring relief in Income Tax
Enough of these unworthy cracks!
'The time draws near the birth of Christ'.
A present that cannot be priced
Given two thousand years ago
Yet if God had not given so
He still would be a distant stranger
And not the Baby in the manger.

John Betjeman, *Advent*, 1955

BEFORE THE 1920S AND 1930S, presents were usually displayed unwrapped, either beneath the Christmas tree or sometimes hung from its branches. However, at the Great Exhibition of 1851, one of the spectacles was a huge steam-powered gift-wrapping machine – the Victorian admiration for new-fangled technology and the mechanisation of simple tasks coming to the fore!

DURING THE SECOND WORLD WAR, rationing meant that presents were often hard to come by. Indeed, one of the most popular Christmas gifts in 1940 was soap! The philosophy of 'make do and mend' extended to Christmas gift-giving, with many magazines and newspapers listing ideas and instructions for homemade presents.

Boxing Day

The day after Christmas is known as Boxing Day (also marked as St Stephen's Day). It was declared an official holiday in England in 1871 and today this bank holiday is usually a time of recovery after the festivities of Christmas, a day when families come together for Boxing Day lunch, the shops begin selling off their Christmas stock at reduced prices and also, traditionally, a sporting day, including football matches, horse racing and fox-hunting. In some places there is even a 'Boxing Day Dip', when people take a dip in the sea despite the cold weather!

Boxing Day's origins are believed to be found in another form of gift-giving, with a variety of theories as to how the day came about. One idea is that the churches would open their alms boxes and distribute the money to those in need the day after Christmas. Also, in the past, tradespeople, apprentices and servants would collect money from their patrons and employers at Christmas-time, putting the money into Christmas boxes, often made of clay. Boxing Day was the day when the earthenware boxes were traditionally smashed open to get the money out. The 1878 Christmas supplement of *Hand and Heart* magazine also notes the tradition of giving Christmas 'boxes' to those in your community who perform some type of service. They admonish the reader to choose their Christmas box recipients wisely – 'the right gift to the right person' – and go on to say: 'We would add a word of caution against the gift of intoxicating beverages to our friends the postman, the policeman and the parcel deliverer. A dozen Christmas Boxes of this kind are enough to rob any man of his character.'

SECRET SANTA is a popular way to exchange gifts in the office, among groups of friends or in large families – it's a good way to curb spending but still participate in the fun of giving. The names of each person in the group are placed in a hat and then drawn out one by one – you become the Secret Santa to the person whose name you have chosen. The gifts can be given totally anonymously, though Secret Santas often reveal their identities during the exchange, and there is usually a spending limit imposed on the gifts.

STOCKINGS

THE TRADITION OF HANGING UP STOCKINGS for Father Christmas or Santa Claus developed in America, brought there by early immigrants from the Netherlands, and the practice had come to England by the mid-19th century. It was possibly based on the Dutch custom where children left their clogs beside the fireplace for St Nicholas on the evening of 6 December (and sometimes Christmas Eve) – they would

put straw in their shoes as a treat for his horse and if they had been good he would leave the shoes filled with sweets and presents; however, if they were bad he would leave the straw behind and place a birch rod in the shoes instead of gifts. This then developed into the use of socks or specially made Christmas stockings, which could be filled with a variety of 'stocking stuffers': small presents, fruit, candies and sometimes coins. Stockings are either put at the end of the bed on Christmas Eve or, as Clement Clark Moore's famous poem tells us, 'hung by the chimney with care'. It is also traditional that

a lump of coal or pile of cinders will be found in the stockings of children who have behaved badly during the preceding year.

117

SIMILAR TO THE DUTCH CUSTOM, children in Italy would leave out their shoes (and stockings) on the eve of Epiphany (5 January) for La Bufana to fill with presents. The legend of La Bufana states that she was an old woman who, one day while sweeping, met the wise men when they were on their way to find Christ. She asked where they were going and they told her that they were following a star to find a new-born child and asked if she'd like to come along with them. She was too busy with her chores so she declined but later realised the significance of the child they were searching for and regretted not joining them. So she spent the rest of her days travelling round, providing gifts for children in the hopes that one of them would be the child she had missed out on seeing with the wise men! Today a toy fair named after La Bufana is set up in Rome's Piazza Navona every year from early December until 6 January.

Santa Claus

...Yes, Virginia, there is a Santa Claus...

(Editorial, New York *Sun*, 21 September 1897)

IN 1897 EIGHT-YEAR-OLD Virginia O'Hanlon wrote to the editor of the New York *Sun*, asking whether Santa Claus existed. Her doubts on the subject had been influenced by her friends telling her that Santa wasn't real and when she asked her father if this was so, he told her to write to the *Sun* because if she saw it in that paper then it must be true! The answering editorial, written by Francis Pharcellus Church, traced the philosophical question of belief and assured her that Santa Claus did exist, concluding with the strong words that exactly sum up the spirit of the character:

No Santa Claus! Thank God! He lives, and he lives forever. A thousand years from now, Virginia, nay, ten times ten thousand years from now, he will continue to make glad the heart of childhood.

Before the development of the modern Santa Claus – the red-suited jolly figure that is so well known today – there were other characters associated with Christmas-time, such as St Nicholas, Father Christmas and even 'the spirit of Christmas', an early 19th-century personification depicted as a merry-making old man bearing a glass (presumably of alcohol) in one hand.

St Nicholas, a 4th-century bishop of Myra (in modern-day Turkey), is firmly associated with Christmas-time, though his saint day is actually 6 December, the day when he is reputed to bring gifts to children. He was revered for his kindness and generosity, and several of the stories that arose around him reflect these qualities. One legend – and one that can perhaps be seen as an influence on the Christmas stocking tradition – tells how he anonymously provided the dowries for the three daughters of a poor Christian man by throwing bags filled with gold coins either through the window or down the chimney, where they landed in the clean stockings hung up to dry by the fire. The legends surrounding him – along with his depiction as a white-bearded and robed figure (albeit with a bishop's mitre and crosier) – seem to have influenced the later figures of Father Christmas and Santa Claus.

The character of Father Christmas has been familiar in England since at least the medieval period, though he has been known under a variety of names including Sir Christmas, Mr Christmas, Lord Christmas, Old Christmas and simply Christmas. A personification of

A mural of Father Christmas by wartime evacuees at Sayers Croft, Surrey.

119

the goodwill and cheer of the season, he was depicted as a jolly, bearded man wearing a fur-lined robe and was often a character in mummers' plays, medieval carols and masques (courtly entertainments) during the 16th and 17th centuries. The figure of Father Christmas was also used by the Royalists in their pamphlets defending the celebration of Christmas during the Puritan ban of the holiday from 1644. During the 19th century, Father Christmas continued to be shown in illustrations wearing a robe (of various colours) and with greenery adorning his head. The Ghost of Christmas Present from Charles Dickens' *A Christmas Carol* certainly seems to have been influenced by this developing Father Christmas and his association with good cheer. There is also some speculation that Father Christmas had a precursor in the Norse god Odin, who was sometimes shown with a white beard and wearing a blue hooded robe or cloak; he was said to travel throughout the world at midwinter, riding a horse or eight-legged goat and bringing presents or punishment, depending on what each recipient deserved.

It was during the 19th century that the traditional figure of Santa Claus really came about in America, merging many of the qualities found in his precursors, St Nicholas and Father Christmas, into a secular character primarily aimed at children. The name itself seems to be a development from Sint Nicolaas – brought to America by Dutch immigrants – which became Sinterklaas, later Americanised to Santa Claus. He was mentioned in Washington Irving's *History of New York* (1809), but the modern form of this character was first described in the poem *A Visit from St Nicholas* (also known as *'Twas the Night Before Christmas*) by Clement Clarke Moore, a professor of Oriental and Greek literature at Columbia University in New York.

...Down the chimney St Nicholas came with a bound.
He was dressed all in fur, from his head to his foot,
And his clothes were all tarnished with ashes and soot;
A bundle of Toys he had flung on his back,
And he looked like a pedler just opening his pack.
His eyes – how they twinkled! his dimples how merry!
His cheeks were like roses, his nose like a cherry!
His droll little mouth was drawn up like a bow
And the beard of his chin was as white as the snow;
The stump of a pipe he held tight in his teeth,
And the smoke it encircled his head like a wreath;
He had a broad face and a little round belly,
That shook when he laughed, like a bowlful of jelly.
He was chubby and plump, a right jolly old elf,
And I laughed when I saw him, in spite of myself...

Moore wrote this poem for his children in 1822 and it was published anonymously (and without permission) in 1823 in a newspaper in Troy, New York. Santa Claus was further popularised in the American author L Frank Baum's 'biography', *The Life and Adventures of Santa Claus*, published in 1902.

However, it was with the engravings of Santa Claus by Thomas Nast for the American magazine *Harpers Weekly* that the 'jolly old elf' came to life in the form that is recognisable to people all over the world today. Nast's first engraving was titled 'Santa Claus in Camp' and was for the 3 January 1863 issue. This illustration showed Santa and his reindeer delivering presents to Union soldiers during the American Civil War. He continued to depict Santa Claus in other illustrations for *Harpers* throughout the 1860s.

Other early illustrations of Santa Claus show him wearing a variety of colours. By 1910 the traditional red garb was commonplace, though some wrongly believe that the red associated with Santa Claus actually came about in 1931 through the Coca-Cola company, who started using yearly representations of Santa in their advertising campaigns. Haddon Sundblom depicted him as a white-bearded figure wearing a red suit – supposedly the red used in the Coca-Cola labelling – and big black boots, leading to urban legends that the company had actually invented Santa Claus!

Throughout the years a whole story has evolved around the figure of Santa Claus. He is said to live at the North Pole with Mrs Claus and there have been poems and songs focusing on her role and character too. Santa keeps a list of all the children in the world, recording who is 'naughty or nice' – and certainly a lot of children are remarkably good around the holiday season in a last ditch attempt to get onto the 'nice' list! While early on Santa supposedly crafted all of the toys himself, the idea of a workshop full of elves making the toys later developed. Modern media often makes a joke of the elves with images of a disgruntled elf workforce going on strike, elves playing pranks on Santa Claus to his eternal resignation and even a Hollywood movie about a human child raised by Santa's elves.

St Nicholas is not only the patron saint of children, but also sailors, merchants, judges, bakers, pawn-brokers, murderers and thieves!

In some parts of Europe, the Christmas gift-giver was known as 'Christkindlein' or 'the Christ child'. He often travelled with a St Nicholas-like figure or was accompanied by a dwarven helper. His name later developed into Kriss Kringle, which has sometimes been used as another name for Santa Claus.

You can learn how to be Santa Claus! The Charles W Howard Santa Claus School was established in 1937 and is the oldest and longest running school of Santa Clausing. It is located in Midland, Michigan, USA, where it teaches its students how to portray Santa Claus through appearance and actions, and also what they need to know about Santa's story in order to answer the multitude of questions posed by children on all Santa-related topics.

———

The traditional association between reindeer and Lapland has led to the popular belief – officially asserted by Finland in 1927 – that Santa Claus lives in Lapland today. His post office is said to be in  Rovaniemi and approximately 600,000 letters to Santa Claus are sent there every year. Travel companies even organise trips to visit Santa in Lapland at Christmastime. The small town of North Pole, Alaska, also receives hundreds of thousands of letters addressed to Santa Claus. If the children provide a return address, they usually receive a reply from one of Santa's elves or helpers, with a North Pole postmark on the envelope!

———

NORAD, a US-Canadian military organisation that deals with aerospace defence over North America, has tracked Santa Claus for over 50 years. Using radar, satellites, Santa Cams and a jet fighter aircraft, NORAD can track Santa from the moment he leaves the North Pole on Christmas Eve. The Santa Tracking Operations Center answers children's phone calls and emails, letting them know Santa's whereabouts, and also provides updates on their website: www.noradsanta.org.

———

Santa's reindeer

...When, what to my wondering eyes should appear,

But a miniature sleigh, and eight tiny reindeer,

With a little old driver, so lively and quick,

I knew in a moment it must be St Nick.

Moore's 1822 poem *A Visit from St Nicholas* gives us the first mention of reindeer pulling a toy-laden sleigh. He goes on to tell us the names of each of the reindeer – Dasher, Dancer, Prancer, Vixen, Comet, Cupid, Donder and Blitzen – and describes how they flew through the sky with the sleigh coursing behind them and landed on the roof so that St Nick could come down the chimney with his presents.

Notable by his absence in these lines is Rudolph, the famous red-nosed reindeer. This is because he is a late addition to the Santa Claus story. In 1939 Montgomery Ward, an American department store and mail-order business, asked advertiser Robert L May to create a Christmas tale as part of their holiday marketing campaign. He wrote the story of Rudolph, a reindeer with a glowing red nose that helped him to lead the eight other reindeer

while pulling Santa's sleigh in bad weather. The story proved a huge success – the year it was written over 2,400,000 copies of the story were sold. May's brother-in-law Johnny Marks turned the story into a song and it was recorded by Gene Autry in 1949, with several other singers covering it over the years. Rudolph captured the public's imagination and in 1964 he appeared in a cartoon on American television, which became one of the longest running TV specials on the American networks. The BBC later created the character of Robbie the Reindeer, Rudolph's son, in two animated Christmas specials (*Hooves of Fire* and *The Legend of the Lost Tribe*) aired for Comic Relief.

Interestingly, despite assumptions that Santa's reindeer are male, many would assert that they must actually be female – all the illustrations show them with antlers and it is the females that keep their antlers over the winter months.

MUMMERS

To shorten winter's sadness,
See where the folks with gladness
Disguised all are coming,
Right wantonly a-mumming.
Fa la.

Robert Chambers, from *Book of Days*, 1869

THE MUMMERS AND THEIR PLAYS were an important facet of the
Christmas celebrations in the past. Like the Lord of Misrule (*see*
pp 130–1), there are possible antecedents in the role reversals of the
Roman Saturnalia as the mummers took on various disguises and
played different comedic roles. It also probably has some relation to the
early Christian mystery or miracle plays, though mummers' performances were not necessarily religious, even at Christmas-time. A popular
tradition from the medieval period, mumming was also a favourite

Christmas entertainment in the 18th and early 19th centuries, and is a tradition that continues in some places today – for instance mummers' performances are seen in many places in Britain on 26 December and a Mummer's Parade, participated in by thousands, is held in Philadelphia, Pennsylvania, USA, on New Year's Day.

The central plot of most mumming plays involves one character killing another, who is then resurrected. The characters include a hero, a villain and the doctor who restores the dead to life. Father Christmas – usually recognised by his wassail bowl and the greenery adorning his costume – also sometimes had a starring role, as did other minor characters such as Beelzebub and Oliver Cromwell. One of the most common mumming plays was a performance of *St George and the Dragon*, though many of its elements seem to bear no relation to the actual legend of St George! The basic plot sees St George killing the 'Grand Turk' or the 'Turkish Knight', who is then miraculously brought back to life by the doctor.

During the medieval period mummers took their plays to the towns as well as performing for the nobility. Edward III is thought to have introduced mumming as a courtly entertainment at Christmas and in 1400 Henry IV spent the holiday at Eltham Palace where he enjoyed the mumming performance of 12 aldermen and their sons. Interestingly, in 1414 a Twelfth Night mumming performance at Eltham was planned as the cover for a coup against Henry V by a group of Lollards, but it was discovered and foiled before the play was performed. During the reign of Henry VIII, an ordinance was actually passed against mumming – if mummers were caught, they could be arrested, put in jail for three months and fined. This was due to the fact that some mummers were using their disguises to help them commit crimes!

———————

MUMMERS were called guisers or guizards in Scotland.

———————

PANTOMIMES

WITH CRIES OF 'HE'S BEHIND YOU!' and the showering of sweets from the stage, pantomimes are one of the most well-known and well-loved Christmas entertainments. Its origins lie in the medieval '*commedia dell'arte*', a type of Italian theatre that was possibly derived from ancient Roman performances by a single masked dancer called Pantomimus. These *commedia dell'arte* performances were improvisational and consisted of a troupe of actors who travelled round entertaining their audience by acting out a variety of stories based on universal themes such as love, jealousy or old age. These types of plays had come to Britain by the 16th century.

As with many other Christmas traditions, the pantomime was really embraced and developed during the Victorian period. At first it was more like a variety show and included all sorts of entertainers and acts such as juggling, acrobatics, comedians and singers. These days pantomimes tend to focus on a particular story – often a traditional children's tale – such as *Cinderella*, *Jack and the Beanstalk*, *Puss in Boots*, *Sleeping Beauty* and *Aladdin*.

The cast of *Mother Goose* pose for a press call at Stoke-on-Trent in 2005.

The character Harlequin was popular in Victorian productions; based on the Italian Arlecchino, he was introduced to England in the 18th century, though he was called Lun (from Lunatic) at the time. The Victorians also introduced Dick Whittington and Robin Hood as pantomime heroes. Role reversal, perhaps hearkening back to the pagan and earlier Christmas celebrations that embraced the topsy-turvy, is also a common theme in pantomimes; 'dames' such as Widow Twankey in *Aladdin* are usually played by a man, while the 'principal boy' is played by a girl. Today many pantomimes have celebrity guest stars, including Sir Ian McKellan who played Widow Twankey at the Old Vic in London in 2005!

Augustus Harris – manager of London's Theatre Royal, Drury Lane, from 1879 – is considered the Father of the Modern Pantomime.

The Nutcracker

In 1816 E T A Hoffman wrote a story called 'The Nutcracker and the Mouse King'. Adapted into a children's tale by Alexander Dumas in 1844 and set to music by Tchaikovsky in 1891–2, the ballet was first performed in England in 1934. Today *The Nutcracker* is a favourite Christmas entertainment.

The Nutcracker tells the story of Clara, who is given a nutcracker in the form of a soldier as a Christmas present. Later that night after all the family have gone to bed, Clara comes out to the Christmas tree to check on her present and falls asleep with it in her arms. Wakened by a noise, she is then threatened by the Mouse King and his mice, who are then fought by the Nutcracker and his soldiers. Both the Mouse King and the Nutcracker die in the ensuing battle, but Clara's tears revive the Nutcracker, who then turns into a prince. He takes her to a magical land where she meets a variety of characters – including the Sugar Plum Fairy, Chocolate, Coffee and Tea – who dance for them, until Clara finally wakes up under the Christmas tree still holding her precious Nutcracker in her arms.

Despite the popularity of *The Nutcracker* today, Tchaikovsky wasn't happy with his composition and didn't really consider it a success!

Role reversal

Role reversal and wearing disguises were common in both the midwinter pagan festivities and the later Christmas celebrations, especially those that grew up around Twelfth Night. During the Roman Saturnalia, one of the main activities was that of role reversal, turning the world topsy-turvy as slaves and masters exchanged places, people wore masks and disguises, and a 'mock king', usually chosen from the freemen, presided over the festivities and issued his commands to the revellers. Supposedly men and women would also interchange their roles at this time.

The Lord of Misrule, a tradition possibly inspired by the Saturnalia role reversals and further developed in the medieval period, was a title given to a minor member of a household by the master of the house. Over the 12 days of Christmas, this 'Lord' would take charge of the proceedings, oversee the various celebrations and punish anyone who did not obey his commands. There were also 'official' Lords of Misrule appointed in royal households in England. Henry VII had a Lord of Misrule and an Abbot of Unreason at Christmas-time. George Ferrers was the royal Lord of Misrule during the short reign of Edward VI – his role was so important that he had his own livery, coat-of-arms and crest! The Lord of Misrule custom effectively ended during the English Civil War and did not really regain a foothold as a Christmas custom after the restoration of the monarchy in 1660. The Bean King was a similar tradition (*see* p 57).

Despite its possibly pagan origins, there was a version of the Lord of Misrule amongst the church clergy during the medieval period – the Feast of Fools (or Asses or Sub-Deacons) which allowed members of the lower clergy to take control of the religious ceremonies over the holiday period. However, quite a few of the higher clergy deplored the pranks, disguises and 'irreverent mimes' that went on. The custom of the 'boy bishop' seems to have replaced the Feast of Fools by the 15th century. It was especially popular in Britain, though it was briefly banned during the reign of Henry VIII and had essentially died out by the end of the Elizabethan Reformation. Observed from St Nicholas' Day (6 December) through to Holy Innocents' Day (28 December), the tradition allowed boy choristers in cathedrals and even some schools a chance to engage in their own processions and festivities. In some cathedrals one of the choristers was appointed as 'bishop' and he led the procession and took charge of parts of the religious services.

I'm dreaming of a white Christmas…

Our modern Christmas has been influenced by popular media over the years with television shows like the *Only Fools and Horses Christmas Special*, films such as *It's a Wonderful Life* and *Miracle on 34th Street*, and contemporary songs becoming part of the holiday tradition. One of the most influential and well-known of these is Irving Berlin's *White Christmas*. Written in 1940, the song was first performed by Bing Crosby on his CBS radio show in 1941 and it quickly became one of the top singles – indeed, over 50 million copies of the single have been sold since it was first recorded! The song was used in Crosby's musical *Holiday Inn* in 1942, when it won an Oscar for Best Original Song, and then again in another of Crosby's musicals – *White Christmas* – in 1954. Since its first recording, it has been covered by artists as diverse as Ella Fitzgerald, The Beach Boys, Billy Idol and Girls Aloud.

JAMES FRAZER (1854–1941) RECORDS in *The Golden Bough* that Roman soldiers stationed on the frontier chose a 'mock king' amongst themselves for the Saturnalia and after he had served in this capacity for 30 days, he was sacrificed to the god Saturn.

Christmas Games

AN ACCOUNT BY JOHN TAYLOR, a Thames waterman, gives us an idea of what the average person enjoyed doing over the Christmas period during the Stuart era – he mentions feasting, dancing, playing cards, singing carols, telling stories and playing games such as hot cockles.

CHARADES

CHARADES IS SAID to have originated in France during the 18th century, later spreading throughout other parts of Europe and England. Early versions of the game focused on elaborate verbal riddles where the participants guessed the syllables of a word or phrase. Winthrop Mackworth Praed (1802–39) even became famous as a composer of the complex riddles used in the game. In 1878 *Hand & Heart's* 24 December issue provided a list of verbal charades to help while away the hours at Christmas-time, giving the answers in the next issue:

> My *first* is equality, my *second* inferiority, and my *whole* superiority. (Answer: Peerless)

> My *first* is a jump, my *second* can jump, and my *whole* is a game of jumping. (Answer: Leap-frog)

Other versions involved complex productions where the participants would dress up and act out the charades. In this version of the game – much like our modern version of charades – the players would act out the syllables and then the whole word. During the Victorian period, these were often quite elaborate performances with a stage and backdrops being set and several parts being played for the audience. While charades was not solely played during the holidays – it was a fashionable pastime described in Jane Austen's *Emma* and William Makepeace Thackeray's *Vanity Fair* – it did become a popular Christmas tradition.

CHARADES WAS SOMETIMES PLAYED during Twelfth Night celebrations. Cards indicating various characters would be put inside the Twelfth Night Cake (*see* pp 57–60) and participants had to act out the character of the card that they found in their slice.

BLIND MAN'S BUFF

THIS GAME HAS BEEN PLAYED from at least the 14th century onwards, and involves one blindfolded player trying to catch the others. Having captured a victim the Blind Man has to guess the identity of his captive – if correct that player takes a turn as the Blind Man.

During Ebeneezer Scrooge's foray with the Ghost of Christmas Present, he observes a party at his nephew's house, where the partygoers are playing this game:

There was first a game at blind-man's buff. Of course there was. And I no more believe Topper was really blind than I believe he had eyes in his boots... The way he went after that plump sister in the lace tucker, was an outrage on the credulity of human nature. Knocking down the fire-irons, tumbling over the chairs, bumping against the piano, smothering himself among the curtains, wherever she went, there went he.
Charles Dickens, *A Christmas Carol*, 1843

SNAPDRAGON

IN THESE HEALTH-AND-SAFETY-CONSCIOUS DAYS it is hard to imagine a game where the object was to pluck currants from a bowl of flaming brandy and pop them in your mouth while they were still sizzling and burning. However, just such a game was popular in England from

the 16th to 19th centuries. Known as Snapdragon, it became a favourite after-dinner entertainment at Christmas during the Victorian period. Correspondents of the time described it with ill-concealed glee and one can imagine the darkened room and dancing flames in an account from the *Illustrated London News*: '...The spirit burns, the dish is a lake of fire; and he who can gather the prize from the jaws of peril is welcome to it..."Faint heart never won a plum!"'

It has been debated whether Snapdragon was played solely by adults – especially young people – or was one that could be classified as 'family entertainment'. It doesn't sound like a game that should be played by young children – or adults for that matter – but contemporary illustrations show Victorian families clustered round the shallow flaming bowl, the children seemingly as eager as the adults to get as many flaming currants as possible in their mouths.

Lewis Carroll's creation in *Through the Looking-Glass* (1871) of a 'snap-dragon-fly', whose body was a plum pudding with holly-leaf wings and a raisin burning in brandy for its head, illustrates the influence of the game on popular culture. And Snapdragon was also celebrated in contemporary verse:

Here he comes with flaming bowl,
Don't he mean to take his toll,
           Snip! Snap! Dragon!
Take care you don't take too much,
Be not greedy in your clutch,
           Snip! Snap! Dragon!

With his blue and lapping tongue
Many of you will be stung,
           Snip! Snap! Dragon!
For he snaps at all that comes
Snatching at his feast of plums,
           Snip! Snap! Dragon!

But old Christmas makes him come,
Though he looks so fee! fa! fum!
           Snip! Snap! Dragon!
Don't 'ee fear him, be but bold –
Out he goes, his flames are cold,
           Snip! Snap! Dragon!

———————

FLAPDRAGON seems to have been the 'country cousin' of Snapdragon. Especially popular in the south-west of England, one version of this game involved placing a lighted candle in a vessel filled with ale or cider and then drinking it down, trying not to get burnt in the process presumably!

———————

I'll swear him guilty.
I swallow oaths as easy as snap-dragon,
Mock-fire that never burns.
John Dryden, *The Duke of Guise*, 1683

———————

BULLET PUDDING: Jane Austen's niece Fanny wrote to a Miss Chapman in 1804, describing a game called Bullet Pudding (whose description makes it sound a bit like a precursor to Jenga!):

" You must have a large pewter dish filled with flour which you must pile up into a sort of pudding with a peek at top. You must then lay a bullet at top and everybody cuts a slice of it, and the person that is cutting it when it falls must poke about with their noses and chins till they find it and then take it out with their mouths of which makes them strange figures all covered with flour but the worst is that you must not laugh for fear of the flour getting up your nose and mouth and choking you: You must not use your hands in taking the Bullet out. "

HOT COCKLES: Popular from the medieval period and still played during the Victorian era, one player would be blindfolded and then made

A pile of flour is set out on a table at Walmer Castle, Kent, ready for a game of Bullet Pudding.

to kneel on the floor with his or her head laid in the lap of another player. As the blindfolded player held one hand behind the back with the palm up, the other players would slap the hand and he or she must guess who has slapped them. A letter to the *Spectator*, written by a footman on 28 December 1711, reports that a housemaid that he was in love with slapped him very hard in the head with her shoe while the servants were playing Hot Cockles. He finishes by asking, 'Pray, sir, was this love or spite?'

CHRISTMAS BAG: A large paper bag would be filled with sugar plums and hung from a door-frame or ceiling. The children were then blindfolded and were each given three tries to hit the bag with a long stick, hoping to break it open and shower the group with sweets. Older children might play the game with a bag filled with small presents such as books, pin cushions or beads. At the end of the game another bag is brought in –

secretly filled with flour it gives the group quite a surprise when it is finally broken open!

———————

IN MEXICO a special *piñata*, filled with gifts and sweets, is hung up at Christmas. It is shaped like a seven-pointed star, said to represent the Devil and the seven deadly sins. As with the Christmas Bag, the blindfolded children attempt to hit the *piñata* with a stick, breaking it open to release the sweets. However, there is symbolic meaning attached to this act – it is likened to releasing the blessings that were being held back by the Devil.

———————

Religious Celebration

OF COURSE, Christmas is enjoyed by Christians and non-Christians alike and people of all different religions celebrate the festival. However, the original reason for all the eating, drinking and making merry was to mark the birth of Jesus Christ.

Most of the elements in this section originally evolved in the church or chapel, the traditional centre of Christian worship – manger scenes and carol services for example. Now many of these activities also take place in shops, homes and schools and they have altered along with our ever-changing ethics, culture and the needs of society.

ADVENT CALENDARS

ADVENT IS A TIME OF ANTICIPATION when excitement about Christmas builds up. It begins on the 4th Sunday before Christmas (the Sunday nearest 30 November, St Andrew's Day) and it was originally a period of fasting and meditation. The passing weeks are traditionally marked in churches with an Advent wreath holding three purple candles and one pink one. A candle is lit on each Sunday in Advent with the pink one, symbolising joy, being lit on the third Sunday. Some churches also have a fifth, white candle, which is lit on Christmas Day.

The tradition of Advent calendars is really quite recent. It began in Germany during the 19th century and soon became popular worldwide. An Advent calendar consists of a card with a scene on it and 24 'doors' which are opened each day from 1 December as a countdown to Christmas. When the doors are opened they reveal an appropriate image such as a star, bell etc. By far the largest door, and often a double one, is 24 December which usually shows a picture of the nativity. In recent times, however, the pictures on the outside and inside of many calendars on sale have become secular rather than religious and now many feature favourite television characters and pop idols.

A very popular change of style in the last 30 years has been the introduction of a small chocolate behind each of the doors. But with

139

chocolate or without, Advent calendars are a very special part of Christmas and many children in their 20s and 30s still love the excitement of them – and still expect their parents to provide them!

The Advent Virus
WARNING... WARNING: ADVENT VIRUS

Be on the alert for symptoms of inner *Hope, Peace, Joy and Love*. The hearts of a great many have already been exposed to this virus and it is possible that people everywhere could come down with it in epidemic proportions. This could pose a serious threat to what has, up to now, been a fairly stable condition of conflict in the world.

Some signs and symptoms of *The Advent Virus*:

★ A tendency to think and act spontaneously rather than on fears based on past experiences.

★ An unmistakable ability to enjoy each moment.

★ A loss of interest in judging other people.

★ A loss of interest in interpreting the actions of others.

★ A loss of interest in conflict.

★ A loss of the ability to worry. (This is a very serious symptom.)

★ Frequent, overwhelming episodes of appreciation.

★ Contented feelings of connectedness with others and nature.

★ Frequent attacks of smiling.

★ An increasing tendency to let things happen rather than make them happen.

★ An increased susceptibility to the love extended by others as well as the uncontrollable urge to extend it.

Please send this warning out to all your friends. This virus can and has affected many systems. Some systems have been completely cleaned out because of it.

Anon

THE LITURGY OF ADVENT... helps us to understand fully the value and meaning of the mystery of Christmas. It is not just about commemorating the historical event, which occurred some 2,000 years ago in a little village of Judea. Instead, it is necessary to understand that the whole of our life must be an 'advent', a vigilant awaiting of the final coming of Christ. To predispose our mind to welcome the Lord who, as we say in the Creed, one day will come to judge the living and the dead, we must learn to recognise him as present in the events of daily life. Therefore, Advent is, so to speak, an intense training that directs us decisively toward him who already came, who will come, and who comes continuously.

Pope John Paul II, 18 December 2002

Bell Ringing

THE PEALING OF CHURCH BELLS mark so many things in our lives and their notes match the occasion – deep and sonorous for funerals and war memorial services; sharp and resonant as a warning of danger or as a rallying cry; soft and mellow as a call to prayer; and sweet and joyful for Christmas and wedding celebrations.

These different notes are made by the bells being rung in certain sequences known as 'changes'. There are usually a set of between 3–16 bells in a church tower and these are tuned to a diatronic scale to produce an astonishing variety of notes during change ringing.

The sound of bells seems to provoke intense emotion and it is not surprising that they have been traditionally rung throughout the Christmas period for many centuries. The veritable waterfall of sound as the bells peal out across the country to mark Christ's birth is one of the highlights of the festive season.

142

VOICES IN THE MIST

The time draws near the birth of Christ:
The moon is hid; the night is still;
The Christmas bells from hill to hill
Answer each other in the mist.

Four voices of four hamlets round,
From far and near, on mead and moor,
Swell out and fail, as if a door
Were shut between me and the sound:

Each voice four changes on the wind,
That now dilate, and now decrease,
Peace and goodwill, goodwill and peace,
Peace and goodwill, to all mankind.

Alfred, Lord Tennyson (1809–92)

Christmas Bells

I heard the bells on Christmas Day
Their old, familiar carols play,
And wild and sweet
The words repeat
Of peace on earth, good-will to men!

And thought how, as the day had come,
The belfries of all Christendom
Had rolled along
The unbroken song
Of peace on earth, good-will to men!

Till, ringing, singing on its way
The world revolved from night to day,
A voice, a chime,
A chant sublime
Of peace on earth, good-will to men!

Then from each black, accursed mouth
The cannon thundered in the South,
And with the sound
The Carols drowned
Of peace on earth, good-will to men!

And in despair I bowed my head;
'There is no peace on earth,' I said;
'For hate is strong,
And mocks the song
Of peace on earth, good-will to men!'

Then pealed the bells more loud and deep:
'God is not dead; nor doth he sleep!
The Wrong shall fail,
The Right prevail,
With peace on earth, good-will to men!'

Henry Wadsworth Longfellow (1807–82)

Carols

THE SINGING OF CAROLS is such a fundamental part of the celebration of Christmas that we assume that it must be a centuries-old tradition. And in one way it is. However, the carols we know today really owe their existence to the Victorians, and many of the most famous and best loved carols were written during this period.

The problem was that early carols were really rather jolly and bois-terous numbers invariably accompanied by dancing – indeed the word is reputedly derived from either the Latin *caraula* or the French *carole*, both of which mean dancing rather than singing. The early Christian church frowned upon such frivolous behaviour and so carols were not part of the church services.

A carol is usually a celebration of Christ's birth and the first known book of English carols was compiled by Wynkn de Worde in 1521. In the 17th and 18th centuries groups of singers known as 'Waits' went round the houses on Christmas Eve performing carols. They derived their curious name from the fact that Christmas Eve was known as Watchnight or Waitnight. This custom was related to wassailing (*see* pp 68–71) and of course it ultimately led to the popular current tradition of carol singers who visit households throughout the country in the days leading up to Christmas performing well-loved carols – in return for a charity donation (and mince pies and mulled wine if they're lucky!)

Carols were banned by the Puritans in the 17th century and by the 19th century carol singing was virtually unknown in England. However, thanks to the Victorian enthusiasm for Christmas and the dedicated zeal of people determined to preserve the country's ancient oral tradition, the practice was revived; now Christmas wouldn't be the same without the sound of *O Come all Ye Faithful* floating through the winter air heralding the approaching carol singers, and the carol serv-ice of Nine Carols and Nine Lessons at King's College, Cambridge.

"As ALWAYS IT WAS LATE; as always this was our final call. The snow had a fine crust upon it, and the old trees sparkled like tinsel. We grouped ourselves round the farmhouse porch. The sky cleared, and broad streams of stars ran down over the valley and away to Wales. On Slad's white slopes, seen through the black sticks of its woods, some red lamps still burned in the windows.

Everything was quiet; everywhere there was the faint crackling silence of the winter night. We started singing, and we were all moved by the words and the sudden trueness of our voices. Pure, very clear, and breathless we sang:

> As Joseph was a-walking
> He heard an angel sing,
> 'This night shall be the birth-time
> Of Christ the Heavenly King.
>
> 'He neither shall be borned
> In Housen nor in hall,
> Nor in a place of paradise
> But in an ox's stall...'

And two thousand Christmases became real to us then; the houses, the halls, the places of paradise had all been visited; the stars were bright to guide the Kings through the snow; and across the farmyard we could hear the beasts in their stalls. We were given roast apples and hot mince pies, in our nostrils were spices like myrrh, and in our wooden box, as we headed back for the village, there were golden gifts for all."

Laurie Lee, from *Cider with Rosie*, 1959

———

SILENT NIGHT must be one of the best-loved carols – and it apparently owes its existence to a mouse! The legend maintains that just before Christmas 1818 a mouse took a fancy to the bellows of the organ of the church of St Nicholas at Oberndorf in Austria and happily munched its way through the soft leather. The organ was unusable and there was no chance of repairing it in time for the Christmas services. The priest in charge, Joseph Mohr, was desperate to find some song that could be sung without an organ and he remembered a poem he had written a couple of years earlier. He asked the church organist, Franz Gruber, to read it and, if he thought it was suitable, to compose a tune that could be played on a guitar. Franz thought 'Stille Nacht, Heilige Nacht' was ideal and quickly set the words to music and so the congregation of St Nicholas's had the privilege of hearing this wonderful carol sung for the very first time.

THE TOP TEN FAVOURITE CAROLS in a television poll a few years ago turned out to be (in alphabetical order): *Calypso Carol* (1996); *Hark the Herald Angels Sing* (1739); *In the Bleak Midwinter* (1870s); *It Came Upon the Midnight Clear* (1849); *O Come all Ye Faithful* (18th century, translated 1841); *O Holy Night* (1847); *O Little Town of Bethlehem* (1868); *Once in Royal David's City* (1848); *See Amid the Winter's Snow* (1858); *Silent Night* (1818).

THE EARLY HOURS of Christmas morning – sometimes as early as 3am – is the time for the traditional service of Plygain which still takes place in some churches in Wales. Carols are sung by individuals and groups who each take turns to sing in a completely informal service of praise.

148

Manger Scenes

And she brought forth her firstborn son, and wrapped him in swaddling clothes, and laid him in a manger; because there was no room
for them in the inn.

Luke 2:7

A SIMPLE STATEMENT, but one which over the millennia since it was
written has been interpreted in many different ways. Was the manger
made of wood or stone? Most people assume it was a wooden trough
but at the time of Christ's birth many mangers would have been made
of stone. Was the manger inside the house or inn – many dwellings at
that period also included space for the animals – or was it in an out-
building or cave? Could it mean that the manger was brought into the
house as there was nowhere else to put the baby? Would the baby have
been laid in straw or cloth and was he wrapped in swaddling bands?

Despite all these questions a baby lying in straw in a wooden
manger in a stable has become the traditional image of the nativity.
This is the central element in the miniature scenes that have been a
Christmas custom since at least AD 400 when Pope Sixtus III had one
built in Santa Maria Maggiore Basilica in Rome. Later the manger with
the baby became a feature of Midnight Mass services (*see* pp 153–5).

By the 18th century nativity scenes had become a popular
Christmas tradition in secular as well as religious places. They came in
all shapes and sizes and were often made by skilled craftsmen. Made
from simple wood or sumptuous marble, these three-dimensional
models have a very special place in the celebration of Christmas. As
well as the baby Jesus, Mary and Joseph, the scene invariably includes
shepherds and the wise men (even though the Bible is clear that they
weren't there at the same time), along with oxen and a donkey.
Nowadays, the well-loved and often well-worn figures are pulled out
each Christmas in many homes and churches as a small but potent
reminder of the true meaning of Christmas.

149

ONE OF THE FIRST CAROLS CHILDREN learn is *Away in a Manger*. It was first published in 1885 in a Lutheran Sunday School book and two years later William James Kirkpatrick set the words to music. It was reputedly written by Martin Luther (1483–1546) but that myth probably arose because the carol was originally subtitled 'Luther's Cradle Hymn'. The last verse was added later in 1904 by Dr John McFarland of New York City.

Away in a manger,
No crib for His bed,
The little Lord Jesus
Laid down His sweet head.
The stars in the bright sky
Looked down where He lay,
The little Lord Jesus
Asleep on the hay.

The cattle are lowing,
The Baby awakes,
But little Lord Jesus
No crying He makes.

I love Thee, Lord Jesus,
Look down from the sky
And stay by my side,
Until morning is nigh.

Be near me, Lord Jesus,
I ask Thee to stay
Close by me forever
And love me I pray.
Bless all the dear children
In Thy tender care,
And fit us to heaven
To live with Thee there.

We sate among the stalls at Bethlehem;
The dumb kine from their fodder turning them,
Softened their horn'd faces.
To almost human gazes
Toward the newly Born:
The simple shepherds from the star-lit brooks
Brought visionary looks,
As yet in their astonished hearing rung
The strange sweet angel-tongue:
The magi of the East, in sandals worn,
Knelt reverent, sweeping round,
With long pale beads, their gifts upon the ground,
The incense, myrrh and gold
These baby hands were impotent to hold:
So let all earthlies and celestials wait
Upon thy royal state.
Sleep, sleep, my kingly One!

Elizabeth Barrett Browning (1806–61)

151

———————

IN THE SOUTH OF FRANCE manger scenes are often crowded with hundreds of small clay figures. Known as *santons* these represent the traditional trades and professions of old Provence.

———————

NOW THREE YEARS BEFORE HIS DEATH it befell that he was minded, at the town of Greccio, to celebrate the Birth of the Child Jesus, with all the added solemnity that he might, for the kindling of devotion… he sought and obtained a licence from the Supreme Pontiff and made ready a manger, and bade hay, together with an ox and ass, be brought into the place… The man of God, filled with tender love, stood before

the manger, bathed in tears, and overflowing with joy. Solemn Masses were celebrated over the manger, Francis, the Levite of Christ, chanting the Holy Gospel... A certain knight, valorous and true, Messer John of Greccio, who for the love of Christ had left the secular army, and was bound by close friendship unto the man of God, declared that he beheld a little Child right fair to see sleeping in that manger, who seemed to be awakened from sleep when the blessed Father Francis embraced him in both arms. This vision of the knight is rendered worthy of belief, not alone through the holiness of him that beheld it, but is also confirmed by the truth that it set forth, and withal proven by the miracles that followed it... the hay that was kept back from the manger by the folk proved a marvellous remedy for sick beasts and a prophylactic against divers other plagues.

St Bonaventure, *Life of St Francis of Assisi*, 1263

Midnight Mass

EVER SINCE THE PASSING OF TIME has been marked by clocks, the stroke of midnight has always held mystical significance. It is the moment when ghosts are meant to appear and when the night seems at its deepest and most threatening. But it is also seen as a time of magic when all sorts of amazing and unthinkable things (like pumpkins turning into carriages) really do happen. But above all, it marks the death of the old day and the birth of the new with all its potential promise. So it is not surprising that ancient doctrine states that Christ was born on the stroke of midnight.

The celebration of a special Mass at midnight on Christmas Eve was first performed at Santa Maria Maggiore Basilica in Rome where a nativity scene had been constructed (*see* p 149). It became the first of the three Masses on Christmas Day and was originally known as the Angels' Mass. The highlight of the Midnight Mass was, and in many Catholic places of worship still is, the symbolic arrival of the Christ Child – a representation of the baby paraded with great veneration. The baby in the manger was then placed in an important position and, in some countries, it was the custom for the manger to be gently rocked by the altar boys. Children who couldn't attend the Mass came the next day to see the baby.

153

Today Midnight Mass is celebrated by other denominations as well as Catholics and is one of the most popular and well attended services of the Christian calendar.

IN SWITZERLAND if an unmarried boy or girl stops at nine fountains on the way to Midnight Mass and takes three sips from each, they will find their future spouse waiting at the door of the church.

IN PERU TAMALES ARE EATEN after Midnight Mass. The delicacy consists of a rich sweet or savoury filling wrapped in banana leaves.

THE STROKE OF MIDNIGHT – the first second of Christmas Day – is when the animals reputed to be at the nativity will kneel. This legend inspired this famous poem:

THE OXEN

Christmas Eve, and twelve of the clock.
'Now they are all on their knees,'
An elder said as we sat in a flock
By the embers in hearthside ease.
We pictured the meek mild creatures where
They dwelt in their strawy pen,
Nor did it occur to one of us there
To doubt they were kneeling then.

So fair a fancy few would weave
In these years! Yet, I feel,
If someone said on Christmas Eve,
'Come; see the oxen kneel
In the barton by yonder coomb
Our childhood used to know.'
I should go with him in the gloom,
Hoping it might be so.

Thomas Hardy (1840–1928)

_____

AFTER THE CELEBRATION of Midnight Mass in France many people enjoy a special meal known as *le reveillon* (from the French *reveille* meaning 'to wake'). Restaurants stay open into the early hours of Christmas morning to serve it to customers.

_____

OPPOSITE
The Latin Patriarch of Jerusalem carries the representation of the infant Jesus to the crib set up in the Grotto in the Church of the Nativity, Bethlehem, at the end of Midnight Mass. According to tradition, Jesus was born in the Grotto.

154

Nativity Plays

THERE IS A LEGEND that St Francis of Assissi (1182–1226) devised the first ever nativity play in 1223 in Italy so people could fully understand the story of Christ's birth. His biographer reveals that he did indeed set up a nativity scene with a real ox and ass so that he could use the manger to celebrate the Mass, but there is unfortunately no evidence that this then developed into a play (*see* pp 151–2).

In medieval England many towns had their own individual nativity plays. These were often organised and performed by the trade guilds and focused on different aspects of the story – for example Chester and 'N-Town' mystery plays tell the story from the point of view of a local midwife who witnesses Christ's birth. Some of these plays are still performed today and their intriguing scripts and motley array of characters still have the power to bring home the magic of Christmas to those who watch them.

Many primary schools perform their own, often specially written, nativity plays enchanting their audiences of parents, grandparents, family and friends. Shepherds in tea-towel headdresses, angels with

tinsel-edged paper wings; ox and ass in painted masks and baby Jesus
in the form of a plastic doll carry on the long tradition. But today's
multicultural society also means that a number of schools prefer to
mark Christmas in a different, and more appropriate, manner for
their pupils.

———————

This the month, and this the happy morn,
Wherein the Son of Heaven's Eternal King,
Of wedded maid and virgin mother born,
Our great redemption from above did bring;
For so the holy sages once did sing,
That he our deadly forfeit should release,
And with his Father work us a perpetual peace.

John Milton, from *On the Morning of Christ's Nativity*, 1629

———————

Further Reading

Anon 1740 *Christmas Entertainment*. London: Field & Tuer, Ye Leadenhalle Presse

Anon 1861 *Peter Parley's Annual*. London: Darton & Co

Brown, Cameron 2005 *Christmas: Facts, figures & fun*. London: AAPPL Artists' and Photographers' Press Ltd

Carter, Simon 1997 *Christmas Past, Christmas Present: Four hundred years of English seasonal customs 1600–2000*. London: Geffrye Museum Trust Ltd

The Catholic Encyclopedia, New Advent website (http://www.newadvent.org/)

Chambers, Robert 1869 *The Book of Days* (http://www.thebookofdays.com)

Harrington, Caroline 1989 *A Celebration of Christmas*. London: Viscount Books

Hutton, Ronald 1996 *The Stations of the Sun*. Oxford: Oxford University Press

Irving, Washington 1876 *Old Christmas*. London: Macmillan & Co

John, J 2005 *A Christmas Compendium*. London: Continuum Books

King, Constance E 1999 *Christmas: Antiques, Decorations and Traditions*. Woodbridge: Antique Collector's Club

Lalumia, Christine *Ten Ages of Christmas* (http://www.bbc.co.uk/history/british/ten_ages_gallery.shtml)

Miall, Antony and Miall, Peter 1978 *The Victorian Christmas Book*. London: J M Dent & Sons Ltd

Pickles, Sheila, ed 1989 *Christmas: Penhaligon's scented treasury of verse and prose*. London: Pavilion Books Ltd

Row, Doc and Robson, Carolyn 1994 *Midwinter: An education resource pack for the winter term on British traditions*. London: English Folk Dance and Song Society

Valentine, Mrs, ed 1869 *Games for Family Parties and Children*. London: Frederick Warne and Company

Weightman, Gavin and Humphries, Steve 1987 *Christmas Past*. London: Sidgwick & Jackson

Wyndham Lewis, D B & Heseltine, G C 1928 *A Christmas Book*. London: J M Dent & Sons Ltd

158

The Geffrye Museum

THE GEFFRYE MUSEUM is one of London's most friendly and enjoyable museums. Its setting is in the former almshouses of the Ironmongers' Company, delightful 18th-century buildings with attractive gardens. The museum presents the changing style of the domestic interior, shown through a series of period rooms.

Every year since 1989, the museum has mounted a special exhibition called 'Christmas Past', which highlights the seasonal traditions, rituals and decorative styles seen in English homes throughout the ages. The period rooms are decorated as authentically as possible, based on original, ongoing research, and each year the public programme highlights a different theme from the exhibition.

Many regular visitors feel that the Geffrye is at its most magical during December, commenting that the festive decorations in some of the rooms create a sense of longing and memories of their own Christmases past. For others, the displays provide inspiration for the introduction of new decorations and rituals in their own homes. But for some, the exhibition is simply a welcome relief from the high street and from the pressure to shop, cook, entertain and 'be happy'.

THE GEFFRYE MUSEUM
Kingsland Road, London E2 8EA
Tel: 020 7739 9893
Recorded information: 020 7739 8543
Information desk:
info@geffrye-museum.org.uk
Bookings:
bookings@geffrye-museum.org.uk

The Geffrye Museum is open:
Tuesday– Saturday (10am–5pm), Sunday and Bank Holiday Mondays (12–5pm).
It is closed on Mondays (unless a Bank Holiday), Good Friday, Christmas Eve, Christmas Day, Boxing Day and New Year's Day.

Acknowledgements

Several people have been very helpful in the production of this book, in particular Peter Williams who provided many extraordinary and interesting old publications, scrapbooks and images that he unearthed for us from all sorts of unlikely sources. James Davies and Peter Williams have provided us with wonderful and festive modern images and worked tirelessly and without complaint during our cookery and Geffrye Museum photoshoots. The Geffrye Museum kindly gave us access to their Christmas Exhibition in 2005 and we are very grateful for their support and help, and we would especially like to thank Nancy Loader. Caroline Newton kindly provided her home and cooking skills for our Christmas cookery photoshoot.

In our search for suitable archive images we were helped by Nigel Wilkins, Ian Leith and Keith Austin. We gratefully acknowledge the advice on theological and historical questions that we received from David Gregson at www.ewtn.com, Rabbi Lazer Danzinger at www.chabad.org, Dr Martin Henig, Sally Mewton-Hynds at Walmer Castle and Dr John Pearce.

We would also like to thank Dr Gail Radcliffe for commenting on the text, Adèle Campbell for editing and support; Rob Richardson for his encouragement; Adam Stinson and Derek Edwards for their help with the jacket design. Last but not least, Andrew Barron at thextension provided the stunning design that has made this book such a visual treat.

160

Credits

The extract from *Cider with Rosie* on p 146 is reprinted by permission of PFD on behalf of the Estate of Laurie Lee. © Laurie Lee 1959. The extracts from Sir John Betjeman's poem *Advent* on pp 110 and 114 are © John Betjeman by kind permission of the estate of John Betjeman.

The illustrations in this book are reproduced by kind permission of: Bridgeman Art Library: 18 (St Peter's, Vatican, Rome, Italy), 35 (Private Collection, The Stapleton Collection), 81 (Fitzwilliam Museum, University of Cambridge, UK); © British Library Board. All Rights Reserved (E684.1): 22; George Bunn: 156; Corbis: fc; The Dairy Council: 50; © English Heritage: bc, 2, 13, 29, 38, 41, 45, 53, 58, 68, 70, 72, 83, 89, 91, 94, 99, 101, 102, 105, 106, 109, 111, 113, 114, 115, 117, 119, 123, 141, 144, 148; © English Heritage.NMR: 37, 51, 152; Reproduced by permission of English Heritage.NMR: 6, 26, 33, 34, 39, 92, 107, 118, 120; © English Heritage Photo Library: 14, 84, 136, 143; The Geffrye Museum: 55, 63, 159; Getty Images: 15, 24, 42, 47, 49, 61, 64, 76, 79, 85, 86, 88, 96, 125, 126, 128, 129, 155; Ley Hill School Parents' Association: 103b; Mary Evans Picture Library: 19, 23, 56, 57, 60, 71, 90, 100, 103t, 108; René Rodgers: 11, 67, 116, 138, 150; © Visit Britain: 30; and Peter Williams: 28.

The following illustrations were taken from: *The Girl's Own Book*: 137; *Hand and Heart*, 26 September 1879: 46; *Hand and Heart*, Christmas Supplementary Number 1879: 95; *Peter Parley's Annual*, 1861: 110, 132, 134; and *Punch*, 29 December 1888: 69.

Every effort has been made to trace copyright holders and we apologise in advance for any unintentional omissions, which we would be pleased to correct in any subsequent edition of this book.